BUILDING A FUTURE COUNTRYSIDE

T0346758

ARCHITECTURE
CHINA

CONTENTS

Tourism

Installation -

Xinzhai Coffee Manor
Sectional Model
/ Hua Li

Project -

Lujangba Xinzhai Coffee Manor
/ Hua Li
Ruralation Shenaoli Library
/ Zhang Lei
Lostvilla Boutique Hotel in Yucun
/ Naturalbuild
Jianamani Visitor Center
/ Atelier TeamMinus
Hotel of Septuor
/ temp architects
Beyond Mogan Mountain
/ Jin Jiangbo

Community

Installation -

An Old-new House:
Recycling The Rural
/ Rural Urban Framework

Project -

Angdong Hospital
/ Rural Urban Framework
Xinchang Village Central
Kindergarten
/ Atelier Deshaus
Lukou Grameen Village Bank
/ Zhu Jingxiang
Chaimiduo Farm Restaurant
and Bazaar
/ Zhao Yang
Shimen Bridge
/ Xu Tiantian
Zhongguan Village Tongzi
Pedestrain Bridge
/ Fu Yingbin

Future

Installation -

In Bamboo Roof Model
/ Philip F. Yuan

Project -

In Bamboo
/ Philip F. Yuan
Cloud Village
/ Philip F. Yuan
Taobao Village, Smallacre City
/ Drawing Architecture Studio
Shitang Internet Conference Center
/ Zhang Lei

Rural Futures: Challenges and Opportunities in Contemporary China

Zhang Xiaochun | Associate Professor, Tongji University
Li Xiangning | Professor, Tongji University

Urban and rural are like two faces of a coin. Against the backdrop of urbanization and globalization, development in both rural and urban senses is today marked by a combination of prosperity and adversity. Here in the 21st century, the current state of cities and the trajectory of their development are subject to endless questioning; some even believe that the countryside offers new possibilities for social development. For some time, a number of architects and researchers have begun focusing their efforts on rural issues. In his "Countryside" talk delivered in November 2016 at China Central Academy of Fine Arts, Rem Koolhaas remarked that the increasing migration of people towards cities has led to a hollowing out of rural areas, which constitute 98 percent of the world's land compared to just two percent for cities. Koolhaas also contrasted the ways in which different countries are addressing the problems that the countryside faces.

In China, the situation presents itself in its own unique way, corresponding to the country's particular circumstances. China has enjoyed marked progress in both industrial development and urban infrastructure, yet population figures and land distribution show that agriculture remains the foundation of China's prowess, and even today the country is comprised of "cities surrounded by villages." To say that the countryside is the ground on which China was established and the very foundation of its existence would be no exaggeration.

In the 1920s and '30s, the traditional relationship between China's cities and countryside gradually fell out of kilter: the countryside began to occupy a position of relative weakness, even decline. One cause was the industrial and urban institutional developments heralded by modern times; the other was the country's lagging rural economy. Later, in an attempt to save the countryside, China unveiled a campaign of wide-reaching influence that was to build up rural regions. Yet over the past three decades of rapid industrialization, development in China's countryside has fallen behind, and rural areas have even become burdened with some of the negative aftereffects of urbanization, such as environmental issues, the dwindling value of agricultural production, and the "hollowing out" of villages. In the countryside, both production systems and social structures have been damaged to some degree, which has weakened the countryside's allure. Urban-rural development in modern-day China has come face to face with a question of extreme gravity: How can we bring sustainable, new development to the countryside?

Yet at the other end of the spectrum, cities, too, have faced their own, incessant critique. With dense forests of reinforced concrete, congested traffic, food and air pollution, soaring house prices, and a blistering pace of life, cities are a source of apprehension. This apprehension is prompting people to reexamine urban spaces and shift their gaze towards the countryside.

This shift is by no means a blind choice borne of a lack of other options. Flicking through the pages of China's history books, one will see that the special relationship between city (cheng) and countryside (xiang) is not one of complete diametric opposition. The countryside is not merely a powerhouse of agricultural production. To some degree, it is also the carrier of Chinese agrarian civilization.

It is the homeland. It is the belt that connects us to our ancestral homes. From words and phrases built around the character *xiang*, like *jiaxiang* ("hometown"), and *beijing lixiang* ("to leave one's home"), one can see that this character has forever held a unique place in people's hearts.

But the urban-rural dichotomy brought about by unceasing urbanization and the division between city and countryside has led to a shift in traditional notions of *cheng* and *xiang*. A rift has emerged. Reflecting upon cities and countryside is in essence a reflection upon this very rift. The notion of *xiangchou*, a word similar to, yet more evocative than "homesickness," is perhaps an expression of the yearning to bridge that gulf and return to one's homeland—a homeland that may no longer exist.

As of 2016, a total of 1.59 trillion renminbi has been invested into development of villages and towns around China. Of that sum, 832 billion renminbi (52.3 percent) has gone to villages; 1.19 trillion renminbi (74.7 percent) has gone to building properties in villages and towns, with completed construction area totaling 1.06-

billion square meters.[1] These figures demonstrate the colossal scale of capital being pumped into the countryside, a brand new hotspot of construction in modern-day China. There are similarities to the country's last three decades of divisive urban development, where cities have become something of a testing ground for international architecture, offering developmental and analytical case studies that have been impossible to imitate anywhere else in the world. The sheer scale and shocking speed at which China is building up its countryside suggests we may soon bear witness to a rural rendition of the country's urbanization development. Perhaps the vast countryside is set to become an experimental plot for architects and designers?

When researching construction practices in the countryside, one must first acknowledge the challenges that rural construction faces: first, the simplistic copy and paste of urbanization's rough-and-ready approach onto the countryside; second, the simplistic treatment of the countryside as some kind of nostalgic utopia or "Peach Blossom Spring;"and third, the simplistic vision of the countryside as a dumping

ground for capital and an arena for monetizing homesickness. At the same time, one must also address the opportunities within rural construction: the flow of capital, evolution of technology, and new economic methods heralded by globalization, changes and advancements in rural production methods that have impacted the way people live, and the new possibilities that have been provided for rural construction. Could modern countryside develop a new model—one that cannot be found in cities—to guide architectural and social development?

Recent years have seen increasing numbers of architects, planners, and artists travelling to the countryside to take part in the execution of rural construction projects. Fusing specialist skills with the natural environment, culture, manufacturing, ways of life, and buildings of the countryside, architects and artists have paid heed to such factors as the continuation and development of traditional culture and the bonds within agrarian society. This not only suggests great variety in the many types and functions of physical spaces, but also speaks to the new ways by which villagers are becoming involved and the reach—on many levels—of

1. Village Air Reading. © Li Zhenyu
2. Zhang Lei, Ruralation Shenaoli Library. © Yao Li
3. Naturalbuild, Lostvilla Boutique Hotel in Yucun. © Chen Hao

architects' construction projects. Architects' and artists' designs for the countryside have been both pluralistic and localized. At the same time, they have demonstrated meaningful engagement with the modern countryside's rapidly changing industries and the continuation and renovation of social spaces and cultural legacy. All of the above have added a sense of social responsibility to the significance of these projects.

The wave of architects and artists flocking to the countryside is no longer characterized by one-time, individualistic creation within a rural environment. Instead, it emphasizes sustainable contributions to the transformation of the countryside environment, development of the rural economy, continuation of the agrarian way of life, transformation of industry, and even revival of culture. Such objectives are achieved through efforts to propagate construction projects and social events that are multi-perspective and multilayered in nature. Not only do the construction projects of architects or artists working for China's modern-day rural development successfully reconstruct physical environments; to an even greater extent, they

also embody a reconstruction of the very notion of vernacular architecture, thereby prompting reflection upon rural issues. This is a process that at once provides for and learns from the countryside. It is absolutely not merely a passing developmental phase. Rather, it is long-standing economic, social, and cultural phenomenon that has been a long time in the making.

In this exhibition, the future of the countryside in present-day China is mapped out along six vectors:

The countryside will continue to serve its purpose as a place of residence, and at the same time should maintain its original functions of agricultural and artisanal production. In "Dwellings," architect Dong Yugan marries the life ideal of returning to pastoral dwellings with the realities of China's traditional gardens and countryside, building a viewing installation that reproduces the essential elements of rural living: mountains, water, and forests. Similarly, Hsieh Ying-Chun's series of rural homes built around industrial light-gauge steel frames and Dong Gong's renovation of the Captain's

House paint a modern-day portrait of countryside living on many different levels. In "Production," architect Zhang Lei reproduces a traditional pottery space used for firing a type of porcelain known as *chaiyao*, expanding the boundaries of contemporary architectural significance. Xu Tiantian's transformation of a brown sugar workshop in Songyang, Hua Li's bamboo raft factory in Wuyishan, and Chen Haoru and Li Yikao's pig-rearing facility present different paths by which architecture intersects rural industry.

Cultural creativity and the tourism industry offer a new path for rural rejuvenation. In "Culture," architect Liu Yuyang reproduces a small town of cultural creativity centered upon the theme of memory. The art museum designed by Dong Yugan and others, and the rural workshop designed by Atelier Archmixing offer the countryside a way to transmit and nurture contemporary culture. The cultural rejuvenation projects located in Guizhou's vast rural areas, such as those in the Louna and Banwan villages, include works by international architects Ryue Nishizawa and Seung H-Sang. In "Tourism," Hua Li's coffee estate presents a

Xu Tiantian, Shimen Bridge. © DnA Architects

new model that intimately connects the planting, handicrafts, processed production, tourism, and rural culture. The first town in China to focus on tourism, Moganshan's practices are highly representative. There, a great number of architects, including Naturalbuild, have devoted themselves to the realization of housing projects. Through video, Jin Jiangbo offers us a representation of real life in Moganshan.

Returning to the concept of rural futures, we pursue the reconstruction of facilities that serve rural society and models of construction and operation that are future-facing. In "Community," Rural Urban Framework dismantled a rural structure it had built in the Chinese countryside, shipped it to Venice, and reconstructed it as a demonstration of the firm's unique work on modern service infrastructure, such as health centers. Similarly, Xu Tiantian's series of construction experiments in Songyang,

Chen Yifeng's kindergarten, and Zhu Jingxiang's bank all help rural communities build modern service infrastructure. In "Future," architect Philip F. Yuan synthesizes traditional Chinese bamboo weaving with digital design and on-site, rapid assembly of premanufactured parts made by robotic technologies. This marriage offers a highly promising alternative to relying on localization alone. In addition, the rural logistics network on which all these projects rely is visually represented in Drawing Architecture Studio's "Taobao Village, Smallacre City." Zhang Lei's Shitang Internet Conference Center reminds us of the internet's wide-reaching potential for growth within the countryside.

As an external extension of the final "Future" vector, an enormous 3D-printed work by Yuan simulates possibilities for an integration of future technology and rural public spaces.

1. Ministry of Housing and Urban-Rural Development's, "2016 Statistical Report on Urban-Rural Development," published 22 August, 2017. See the official website of the Ministry of Housing and Urban-Rural Development of the People's Republic of China, www.mohurd.gov.cn.

The New Rural Self-Confidence in China and the Global Challenge

Hans-Jürgen Commerell | Director, Aedes Architecture Forum, Berlin

"The problem is that the city thinks it dominates everything it has developed, from state theory in the Greek agora, through universities and cultural institutions, to urban architecture. But as in dialectics, this leads to the other part resisting it."

Rem Koolhaas, translated from Neue Zürcher Zeitung interview, 1 December 2017.

China presenting an installation on the redevelopment of rural regions to an international audience at the 16th International Architecture Exhibition at Venice Biennale shows, the importance of the topic as a global challenge and the relevance of architecture in this major endeavour. While the realized projects and the experiences of the developments are not entirely comparable or transferable to Europe, the presented insights offer a rich source of ideas, strategies, and knowledge. We are excited that the Chinese Pavilion's curator Li Xiangning invited us to join the debate about the built future of the Chinese countryside.

The initiation of the long-term enquiry and network program "Regions on the Rise" at The Aedes Metropolitan Laboratory, Berlin, in 2016 revealed a new chapter in our exchange with China, based on the legendary Aedes exhibition *TuMu* in 2001. During an almost four-week-long travel in September and December 2017, my partner Kristin Feireiss, curator Eduard Kögel, filmmaker Moritz Dirks, and myself, had the opportunity to explore Songyang County, southwest of Hangzhou. There, as a result of a holistic understanding and through the widespread distribution of a new strategy,

the Songyang government together with the Beijing-based architect Xu Tiantian had implemented carefully considered architectural acupunctures following an integrated concept. Instead of focusing on individual projects, the strategy incorporated a larger number of small buildings of different functions related to the local landscape, community necessities and economy, for example a teahouse and a brown sugar factory. Some of these buildings have been refurbished and some have been designed as new entities. Both approaches have already had a positive influence on the local communities and the economies throughout the Songyang Valley.

To provide incentives for the young generation to stay in the countryside or to convince others to return from metropolitan regions, new strategies have been implemented by various actors and stakeholders. These strategies produced new spaces of opportunity, stimulating new economic developments by protecting the identity and character of this specific rural area. From our point of view, this concept is a pioneering example, which would be a much-needed precedent for Europe, where similar problems are immanent.

Aedes and its affiliated Aedes Metropolitan Laboratory share the interest in dualities and interrelations as it occurs in the relationship between the urban and the rural, always seeking to explore what architecture can do to invent new concepts and therefore a new rural confidence and identity.

The rising importance of the hinterland only came into focus after international architects, city planners, the academic community, and real estate industry intensively discussed primarily urban developments and consequences of the increasing urbanization processes worldwide during the last 50 years. It is a well-known and widely communicated fact that 54 percent of the world's population today lives in urban areas, a proportion that is expected to increase to 66 percent by 2050, according to the 2014 revision of the World Urbanization Prospects report by the Population Division of the United Nations Department of Economic and Social Affairs.

These numbers blur the fact that the other half of the population, a little less than 50 percent of these often-quoted statistics, is still living in the countryside. And while experts and

Village Air Reading. © Li Zhenyu

politicians were and still are busy focusing the architectural challenges and opportunities on the rapid urbanization of the cities and metropolitan areas, everyone largely missed the tremendous change that was already taking place in global rural regions on many levels.

General Rural Situation

The definition of rural has many meanings and associations: the cosy villages embedded in a rich natural environment; the romantic retreat for tourists and stressed citizens; the supply corridors between metropolitan areas; satellite-controlled agriculture of unimaginable large scale; but also dried-out or flooded regions from climate change; and poverty in large underdeveloped, neglected countryside around the world. The rural region is no longer only the space of relief for the overpopulated and hyper-densified cities. New modes of connectivity and mobility systems, digital opportunities, Internet of Things, e-business and e-learning, and a healthier living environment are aspects many inhabitants consider advantages of rural areas as a better place to live and work. Economic values are no longer the incentive for a satisfied and fulfilled life. Nature, wholesome food, and a healthy environment for parents and children are increasingly regarded as important living standards in the developed regions of this world.

It cannot be denied that many inhabitants of rural areas are living below the poverty line and would gladly choose the work and income in the dirt and dust of the city over a low-quality life in the country. But if states and societies succeed in drawing higher-income earners to rural areas, country residents will profit from new perspectives and opportunities coming their way too.

Rural Situation in Europe

Rural regions in Europe, for example, have long been a subject of neglect. Over the past six decades, Europe has seen greater integration and cooperation, and has experienced unprecedented economic growth and prosperity. While this happened mainly around the larger cities and metropolitan areas, increasing numbers of people living in the hinterland moved to prospering urbanized zones, wishing to participate in the real and imaginary wealth. The population in rural regions decreased, infrastructure was barely maintained, and entire villages and small towns became abandoned. Especially in Southern Europe, such as Spain, Italy, and Greece, where climate and geo-graphical conditions created additional specific challenges and threats, rural inhabitants gave up because a modernization of agricultural production was to difficult or too expensive, or the young generation left for better education and more interesting jobs in the big cities.While the Northern European countries were able to compensate the misbalance between the rural and metropolitan regions within their national territories due to high industrial production, high export rate and extensive agriculture, all resulting in a high GDP, the European Union had difficulties finding a balance between the north and south.

According to the European ESPON study, urban and rural regions maintain and safeguard the development of the European territory. Their mutual interdependence guarantees balanced progress, which reinforces the joint progress in regional growth. Defining what is urban and what is rural in a European context is not an easy task. This is due to national specificities, which means that in some countries, for example, rural areas may be of urban character. Of the 32 countries that participated in the ESPON study, 40 percent of the population lives in municipalities, in predominantly urban regions; 35 percent live in the intermediate regions close to a city, and 18 percent live in predominantly rural regions. There are significant national variations between urban and rural occupancy; for example, in the Netherlands, 71 percent of the population lives in urban regions compared to only 10 percent in Romania. [1]

Since the 2008 global financial crisis, all achieve-ments have been under threat and, all European nations have been confronted with a problem that could no longer be ignored. Due to the crisis, which already created huge problems in the more industrialized, wealthy regions and within the economic centres, the rural populations across Europe could not accept further neglect and started to revolt. The established political parties were put under pressure. The "forgotten inhabitants" in the peripheries and in the countryside claimed their rights.

Village Air Reading. © Li Zhenyu

Rural Situation in Germany

This is the case in Germany today. Following reunification in 1999, West Germany was confronted with very specific challenges and problems. Integrating the territory and population of the former German Democratic Republic (GDR), an East German region with low urbanization, inefficient or collapsed industry, and huge agriculture areas of low production, proved to be a task for generations. As one of the wealthiest European nations, Germany, was able to manage this societal and economic surgery so far, but the exodus of former GDR citizens to West Germany, and the already existing flow of people from the countryside to the large cites, rang alarm bells. The East German population not only deserted rural regions and villages but also medium-sized towns and smaller cities. Shrinking cities became a new phenomenon in Germany towards the end of the 1990s.

Because of the more balanced climatic conditions in Central Europe, the hinterland in Germany is green, fertile, gentle, and beautiful. Some regions are traditionally known for tourism in summer, others as winter destinations. Many Germans spend their holidays within their own country. Because of their rich heritage, some regions are popular destinations for international tourism, notably with an increasing percentage of tourists from China. But the average everyday-village, regardless if near to or far from an urbanized region, deserves a concept to survive and is desperately seeking solutions to draw in more citizens to become new villagers.

The privatization of federal services such as railways and telecommunications made rural areas victims of profit maximisation towards the end of the 1990s. When selling the broadcast licences to the large private telecom giants, the German government failed to ensure guarantees for an equal distribution of access to this infrastructure. But it has learned from mistakes and regional governments and private partners are slowly reviving closed railway tracks and subsidizing broadband access.

Rural Situation in the Alpine Territory

The Alpine region is another specific European example. In the past, each Alpine valley with acceptable climatic conditions was inhabited and taken care of by populations whose main aim was to keep the living and working environment safe and productive. Nevertheless, in the 20th century, wide areas of the Alps experienced a severe depopulation trend that resulted in an increased difficulty in providing basic services to the local population, thus putting their living standards at risk.

A number of transnational programs have been initiated to install central digital archives and network platforms where data and analyses can be stored and experiences in many sectors and from various initiatives can be shared. The Alpine Space program, a European Territorial Cooperation, is a research network of various institutions and universities across Europe, developing a rich resource of knowledge and links to different fields such as building culture, water management, agriculture, forestry, and

mobility, and offering support in regional smart planning and consultancy strategies for sustainable development and closed-loop economies.[2]

International Rural Concepts

Solutions have been needed on all scales, and from the state to the territory, new promises are made. Over the last decades, extensive analyses have been commissioned and many actions taken to counteract rural migration. Research agencies and programs have been initiated to collate facts and numbers and to offer new strategies.

In Spain, abandoned rural villages were reconfigured to become new homes for migrants from Latin America and Africa, a model that was also considered in Germany to meet the needs of the large migration flow in 2016. In Italy, the water and electricity supply was privatized in many regions with the expectation of a modernization of the inefficient systems. But increasing expenses and low maintenance made people leave the regions. Greece, heavily affected by the financial crisis, was on sale. Not only were harbours, vineyards, airports and railway systems sold to foreign investors, but islands, farmland, and rural tourist destinations were heavily marketed, causing poverty in the countryside.

In Germany, the role of architecture in the redevelopment of rural regions was emphasized. The Federal Foundation of Baukultur (Bundesstiftung Baukultur) was founded in 2006 and became a relevant consultant, mediator, and instigator for progressive and qualified

Village Air Reading. © Li Zhenyu

development in the built environment. The Foundation's work, such as workshops, symposia, competitions, exhibitions, publications, and especially its analysis of rural conditions, made this agency a strong partner for regional governments and small-town councils to create places of social coherence and, contemporary and attractive conditions for the new rural citizen. A significant number of successful planning strategies and redevelopments of villages and small towns in Germany would fill a similar exhibition like the one that is accompanied by this catalogue.

In Austria, the Vorarlberg region, as an Alpine example, is well developed and of high living standard. For decades it has been known worldwide for its small mountain villages where families live and work, but at the same time for very contemporary, sometimes radical modern architecture.

We know other examples of Swiss mountain villages, or regions in Tuscany, Italy, where the historic image has been kept and the owners of heritage-listed houses from larger cities or other countries are living a nostalgic countryside life during the summer. But outside the holiday seasons, these villages are empty and hollow. While those new owners are looking for a quiet retreat in a rural environment, they do expect

fast connection into digital networks. If the desired infrastructure is missing, there are no incentives for these new villagers to stay, or for those to return to the countryside for permanent residence and work.

The Role Architecture Can Play

Confronted with the massive and diverse challenges, what role can architecture play to stimulate progress in rural Germany or in the hot and dry provinces of mainland Spain? Can the so-called "Bilbao effect" be created to upgrade the attractiveness of the countryside in Europe, China, or anywhere? Yes and no. Exaggerated romanticism and Disneyfication with regards to a revitalization of historic villages and small towns can create a source of income but not an authentic and sustainable place to live and work. Just like a medical overdose, mass tourism can kill well-balanced rural socioeconomic structures and cause segregation amongst the original inhabitants.

Nevertheless, identity can be created with the right balance of inherited building methods and modern design in order to keep an authentic appearance while applying contemporary functions to offer modern living and usage. A coexistence of the new and vernacular is possible.

China Hinterland

The span between the extremes of the global rural phenomena with such different appearances and causes urged the Aedes Architecture Forum and The Aedes Metropolitan Laboratory to consider this an eminent issue to be discussed in a transnational, transdiciplinary manner in a cultural and public context. This will be a focus for the future work of Aedes, always connected to the question of the role architecture and space-production can play to improve the situation.

The Chinese strategies and examples given in the *Building a Future Countryside* exhibition at the Chinese Pavilion for the 16th Venice Architecture Biennale are a substantial contribution on the value of contemporary architecture and its impact on the self-confidence of the new rural citizen.

With Kristin, the Aedes team, and many other friends of our network, we will continue the journey and exploration into the Chinese hinterland. We are curious and excited to experience more great examples of empowerment through architecture and the beauty of rural China.

Sources:
1. ESPON, http://atlas.espon.eu
2. Alpine Space Program, European Territorial Cooperation,
http://www.alpine-space.org/20072013/projects/projects/detail/AlpBC/show/index.html

Building a Future Countryside: Pavilion of China

Li Xiangning | Curator, Pavilion of China,
16th International Architecture Exhibition, La Biennale di Venezia

One of the major challenges facing contemporary built environments is the future of rural development. In China, the countryside has become a new frontier for experiments in this area, and the country is developing its countryside at a speed and scale unseen in the West. Drawn by the promise of boundless opportunity, architects, artists, developers—as well as capital flow—are converging in rural areas across the nation.

The return to pastoral life has long been an ideal of Chinese literary tradition. In modern times, living in rural areas typically involves aspects such as policy, capital, infrastructure, and technology. While modernization and technological progress promise us better lives with modern living conditions, they also, to some extent, sever the link between rural life and tradition. Faced with mass-produced rural housing brought on by urbanization, architects attempt to find a middle ground between tradition and modernization, taking advantage of modern building technology in search of a vernacular connection.

From the great yellow expanse of the Loess Plateau to the watertowns south of the Yangtze, from the vast and abundant plains of northeast China to the green and beautiful farmlands of the south, hundreds and thousands of villages have become sites for industrial development, self-building, and cultural creation. These sites enjoy tremendous opportunities offered by technological innovations, including the internet, logistics systems, and sharing economies. The development of the countryside in contemporary China is unprecedented in both its scale and its approaches. More importantly, this development anticipates a new solution grounded in China's unique conditions.

Building a Future Countryside depicts the rural areas of contemporary China through six episodes: poetic dwellings, local production, cultural practices, agricultural tourism, community reconstruction, and future exploration. This exhibition outlines a **freespace** for opportunity and anticipates future development for the countryside.

The motivation for this exhibition is more than just *xiangchou,* a Chinese term that refers to nostalgia for rural lands. We return to the countryside where Chinese culture originated to recover forgotten values and overlooked possibilities, and from there, we will build a future countryside.

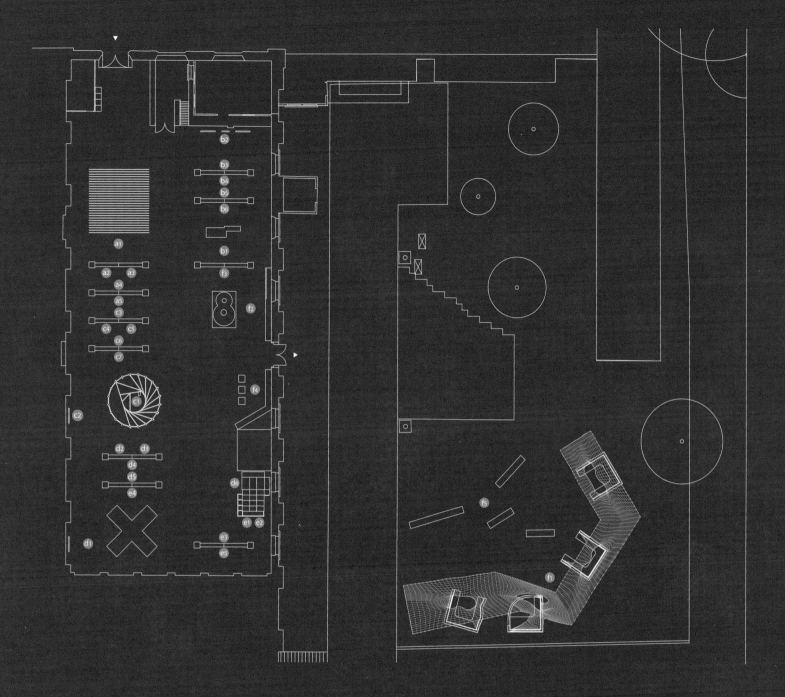

A. Production

(a1) Wood Kiln Bingding - Zhang Lei
(a2) Huateng Hog House Exhibition Hall - Li Yikao
(a3) Taiyang Organic Farming Commune - Chen Haoru
(a4) Songyang Zhangxi Brown Sugar Workshop - Xu Tiantian
(a5) Wuyishan Bamboo Raft Factory - Hua Li

B. Tourism

(b1) Xinzhai Coffee Manor Sectional Model - Hua Li
(b2) Beyond Mogan Moutain - Jin Jiangbo
(b3) Lostvilla Boutique Hotel in Yucun - Naturalbuild
(b4) Hotel of Septuor - temp architects
(b5) Ruralation Shenaoli Library - Zhang Lei
(b6) Jianamani Visitor Center - Zhang Li

C. Community

(c1) An Old-new House: Recycling The Rural - Rural Urban Framework
(c2) Angdong Hospital - Rural Urban Framework
(c3) Lukou Grameen Village Bank - Zhu Jingxiang

(c4) Shimen Bridge - Xu Tiantian
(c5) Zhongguan Village Tongzi Pedestrian Bridge - Fu Yingbin
(c6) Xinchang Village's Central Kindergarten - Atelier Deshaus
(c7) Chaimiduo Farm Restaurant and Bazaar - Zhao Yang

D. Culture

(d1) Cidi Memo, a Town of Memory - Liu Yuyang
(d2) Louna International Architects' Village: Village Vision - Li Xinggang / Seung H-sang / Nishizawa
(d3) Ryue
(d4) Banwan Village Reconstruction - Lü Pinjing
(d5) Huashu Rural Studio - Atelier Archmixing Lianzhou Museum of Photography -
(d6) O-office Architects The Art Museum of Xiaozuo Peninsular and its Garden - Dong Yugan

E. Dwellings

(e1) Mountain Dwelling. Waterside Dwelling. Forest Dwelling - Dong Yugan
(e2) The Guest Quarter and the Courtyard of Eli Villa - Dong Yugan
(e3) Yangliu Village Reconstruction - Hsieh Ying-Chun
(e4) Renovation of the Captain's House - Dong Gong
(e5) Jintai Village Reconstruction - Rural Urban Framework

F. Future

(f1) Cloud Village - Philip F. Yuan
(f2) In Bamboo - Philip F. Yuan
(f3) Shitang Internet Conference Center - Zhang Lei
(f4) Taobao Village, Smallacre City - Drawing Architecture Studio
(f5) Village Air Reading - Li Zhenyu

DWELLI

NGS

居

Returning to a pastoral setting is an ideal in the Chinese literati tradition. Nowadays, dwellings in the countryside have become a far wider issue concerning economics, policies, and community building. While mass-produced rural housing usually severs the link between country life and tradition, architects attempt to rebuild the vernacular connection through space, materials, and the local community.

Dwellings

Dong Yugan creates an installation, **Mountain Dwelling. Waterside Dwelling. Forest Dwelling**, to represent the traditional Chinese dwelling experience among the mountains, along the watersides, and in the forests. Three views are framed to recall the literati ideal of returning to a pastoral setting. The technique of playing with views also appears in his project, **The Guest Quarter and the Courtyard of Eli Villa**, where the ridge of a single-slope roof is used to frame a view towards the hill and the trees. The relationship of a village dwelling to its natural environment is also a consideration of **Jintai Village Reconstruction** by Rural Urban Framework (RUF). If Dong's response to the problem of modern rural livelihood is of romanticism, Joshua Bolchover and John Lin, the two principal architects of RUF, take on a social and ecological perspective. As most houses were destroyed in the Wenchuan earthquake and the following landslides, RUF's design strategy attempts to explore a sustainable model for earthquake reconstruction as well as to rebuild a community. Earthquake reconstruction is also the starting point of HsiehYing-Chun's **Yangliu Village Reconstruction**. A light-gauge steel-frame system similar to the timber framing of local Qiang dwellings' is implemented. The open framework of the design and the construction process allow full participation of villagers as well as maximum engagement with local material and craftsmanship. If both reconstruction projects are shelters against natural disaster, **Renovation of the Captain's House**, by Dong Gong, created an inward haven for an ordinary fishman. Standing on a cliff by the seaside of Huangqi Peninsula, Fujian Province, the house and its added arch structure symbolize a contemporary aspiration on dwelling: to give dignity and decency to the most ordinary people in their everyday life.

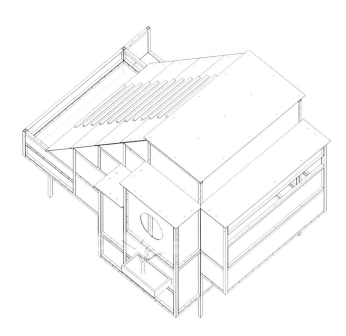

Installation axonometric diagram

MOUNTAIN DWELLING. WATERSIDE DWELLING. FOREST DWELLING

Architect: Dong Yugan
Material: Metal
Size: 2.7x3.1 meters

About 1600 years ago when early Christian buildings started to be constructed on the moor of the European continent, scholarly gentlemen of the Wei and Jin dynasties of China first proposed their ideal model of mountain dwelling. Houses were built among the mountains and forests. About 1000 years ago, when cathedrals were established in the big cities of Europe, literati of the Song dynasty created their new style of mountain dwelling. Houses were moved from among the mountains and forests to the urban area. In China, the poetic essence of these two types of mountain dwelling does not differ because of the locational discrepancies of the urban and suburban areas, and does not vary because of the dissimilarities existing in the religious and the secular contexts. The poetic essence only exists in the form of everyday comfort one can experience by dwelling among the mountains, along the watersides, and in the forests.

The horizontal opening on the southern wall of the installation frames a view of an iron oil can that is set in close proximity, which itself is shaped to form an impression of a mountain—the iron moldings on the oil can help to form an outline that reminds viewers of the mountain's form. The pitched northern wall suppresses

one's view toward a water sink to get a glinted effect that is common for waterside dwellings. The moon window facing east frames the adjacent bonsai plant to indicate the frequently encountered scene of a forest dwelling.

Mountain Dwelling - Beijing Red Brick Museum of Contemporary Art and its Garden

The site has no mountains, no water bodies, no forests. After transforming the preexisting vegetable house into a museum space, my entire interest was shifted to turning the flat land to the north of the building into a mountain. Eventually, the artificial mountain provides places for people to stroll, and comforts of mountain dwelling for a few scattered buildings nearby.

Waterside Dwelling - The Art Museum of Xiaozuo Peninsular and its Garden

The site is adjacent to the sea, and has no mountains and trees. Before transforming an abandoned industrial building of the old medicine manufactory of the village into an art museum, I turned the 100-meter-long ridge of the building into a walkway leading toward the sea. This walkway lures people to the museum café, which was transformed from an abandoned

boiler house. Walking down, one can overlook the sea. The unideal situation of only being able to look afar instead of being able to dwell was ameliorated through turning the nearby filter chambers into a teahouse above a fish pond, sided by a small waterfall.

Forest Dwelling - The Guest Quarter and the Courtyard of Eli Villa

The site has mountains, bodies of water, and forests. It used to be a small hoggery owned by one of my middle-school classmates. I arranged a few guest rooms on the bases of the old pigsties, in order to create an atmosphere, one can experience by dwelling on a mountainside terrace. I laid out a square court amid the miscellaneous trees planted by my client when he was raising pigs, in order to provide a place for forest dwelling. To densify the atmosphere of a mountain dwelling, I used the ridge of a single-slope roof to frame the view of the hill and the trees behind the house intending to lure people to step up to the ridge and stroll along the walkway continuously wrapping the house on different levels.

THE GUEST QUARTER AND THE COURTYARD OF ELI VILLA

Dong Yugan | Beijing University of Civil Engineering and Architecture

Location: Chang Ling Nie Jia, De'an County, Jiu Jiang City, Jiang Xi Province
Architect: Dong Yugan
Design team: Dong Yugan, Zhou Yi, Wang Juan, Zhu Xi
Structure: Reinforced concrete
Area: 60 square meters
Design period: 2 months
Construction period: 12 months

Site plan

The site has mountains, bodies of water, and forests. It used to be a small hoggery owned by one of my middle-school classmates. I arranged a few guest rooms on the bases of the old pigsties, in order to create an atmosphere, one can experience by dwelling on a mountainside terrace. I laid out a square court amid the miscellaneous trees planted by my client when he was raising pigs, in order to provide a place for forest dwelling. To densify the atmosphere of a mountain dwelling, I used the ridge of a single-slope roof to frame the view of the hill and the trees behind the house intending to lure people to step up to the ridge and stroll along the walkway continuously wrapping the house on different levels.

Framed view of the elevated terrace

Erli Villa sunken courtyard

View from roof toward courtyard

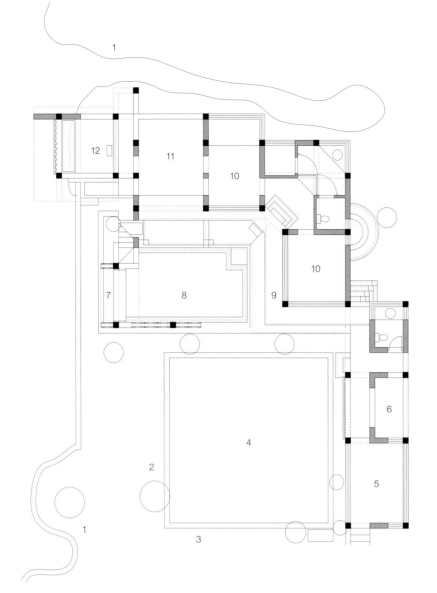

First-floor plan

1. Waterfall
2. Wall table
3. Wall bench
4. Courtyard
5. Card room
6. Canna courtyard
7. Qian xuna
8. Elevated terrace
9. Floating corridor
10. Guest room
11. Tea room
12. Taoguang pavilion

Conceptual section

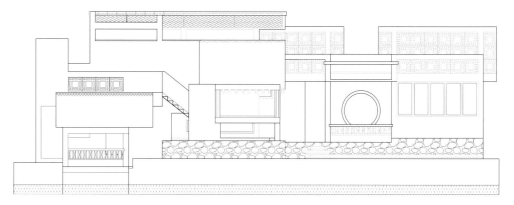

Southwest elevation

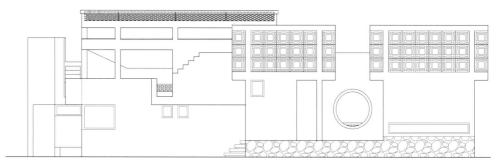

Northeast elevation

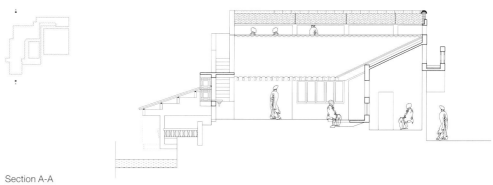

Section A-A

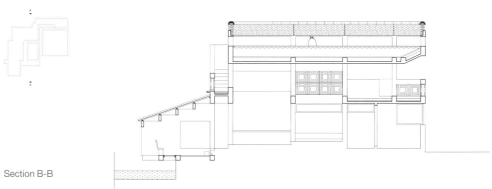

Section B-B

RENOVATION OF THE CAPTAIN'S HOUSE

Dong Gong | Vector Architects

Location: Beijiao Village, Fuzhou, Fujian, China
Architect: Vector Architects
Principal architect: Dong Gong
Project architect: Liu Chen
Construction management: Sun Dongping
Design team: Zhao Dan, Jiang Cunyu, Zhang Zhao
Site architect: Chen Zhenqiang, Zhao Liangliang
Structural and MEP engineering: China Academy of Building Research
Structural consultant: Xiao Congzhen, Du Yixin
Structure: Concrete structure reinforcement (existing masonry concrete structure)
Area: 470 square meters
Design period: January–August 2016
Construction period: May 2016–January 2017
Photography: Zhi Xia, Hao Chen, Vector Architects

Site plan

The Captain's House is located on the southeast end of Huangqi Peninsula, Fujian Province. Over 20 years of use, the damp and erosive nature of the seaside made the existing structure hazardous and caused widespread water leakage. These became the main design issues to be addressed. Furthermore, the captain hoped to add a third floor to the existing structure to accommodate his current lifestyle.

Our design work began with the study of structural reinforcement. After a series of careful comparisons, we decide to add a 12-centimeter-thick concrete wall to the original brick masonry walls. This strategy offered extra potential to create a better quality of space.

Layout

The ability to tear down or relocate the original concrete walls allowed us to rearrange the layout to some extent. Both original bathrooms on the first and second floors were moved from the sea-facing side to the side closest to the

neighboring structure. This allowed the living room, dining room, and master bedroom to enjoy a better view and additional natural light and fresh air.

"Window-furniture" system

The locations and forms of openings also received careful consideration. The new concrete window frames stick out from the outside wall, preventing water from seeping into the window from the surface of the wall during heavy rains. The thickness of these windows was transformed into our "window-furniture" system, in which windows are no longer simple openings, but serve as a medium connecting the outside environment to the interior space.

Vault

We chose a vault as the structural form of the third floor. This form minimizes the possibility of water leakage as it barely allows any rainwater to remain. The vault is directional,

connecting two dramatically different faces of the sea: one a serene bay, the other one a noisy port. This floor was added to serve as a multifunctional living space. It can be used to accommodate visiting family and friends, and functions perfectly as a gym or an activity room as well. In addition, as the captain's family is Christian, this space was also intended for use as a family chapel.

At dusk, the gentle light comes out from the translucent glass blocks. We hope this house will gradually become a vessel for the emotions of the captain's family and give ordinary people the dignity and decency they deserve in their daily lives. This aspect is particularly meaningful given China's current socioeconomic circumstances.

Evening view

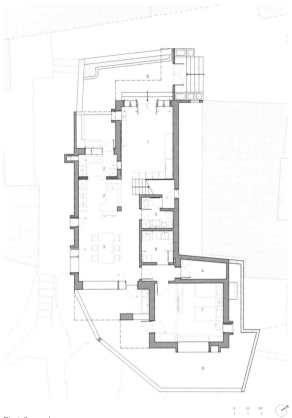

First-floor plan

1. Entrance lobby
2. Kitchen
3. Dining room
4. Storage
5. Bathroom
6. Barrier-free bathroom
7. Barrier-free bedroom
8. Terrace
9. Courtyard

Second-floor plan

1. Boys' bedroom
2. Girls' bedroom
3. Living room
4. Study
5. Bathroom
6. Master bedroom
7. Master bathroom
8. Balcony

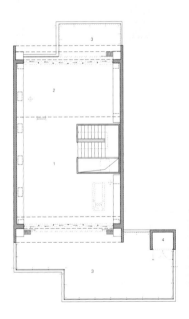

Third-floor plan

1. Multifunctional living space
2. Flexible sleeping space
3. Roof terrace
4. Water tank

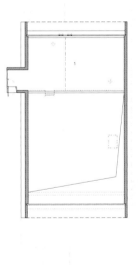

Mezzanine floor plan

1. Multifunctional living space

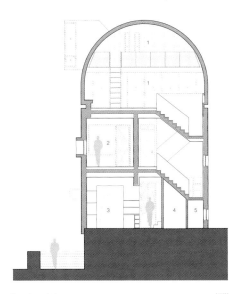

Section 1-1

1. Multifunctional living space
2. Girls' bedroom
3. Kitchen
4. Bathroom
5. Storage

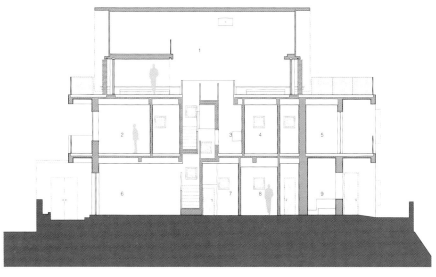

Section 2-2

1. Multifunctional living space
2. Boys' bedroom
3. Study
4. Master bathroom
5. Master bedroom
6. Entrance lobby
7. Bathroom
8. Barrier-free bathroom
9. Outdoor basin

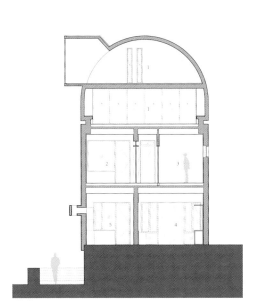

Section 3-3

1. Multifunctional living space
2. Girls' bedroom
3. Bathroom
4. Entrance lobby
5. Kitchen

Exploded axonometric diagram

Southwest elevation

West elevation

Detail

1. Cast-in-place wood formwork concrete
2. Reinforced concrete for structural reinforcement
3. Original brick masonry wall
4. Warm gray texture paint
5. Original stone masonry wall
6. 15x15 mm drip
7. Cherry-wood casement window (open outside)
8. Cherry-wood screen window (open inside)
9. Laminated bamboo flooring
10. Acid-washed granite ground
11. Cherry-wood furniture
12. Matte white paint
13. Matte white paint ceiling

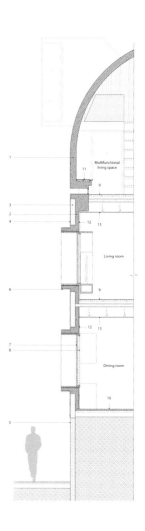

1. Multifunctional living space
2. Living room
3. Girls' bedroom

JINTAI VILLAGE RECONSTRUCTION

John Lin + Joshua Bolchover | Rural Urban Framework

Location: Sichuan Province, China
Architect: Joshua Bolchover and John Lin, Rural Urban Framework
Landscape design: Dorothy Tang, The University of Hong Kong
Project team: Ashley Hinchcliffe, Huang Zhiyun, Ip Sin Ying, Eva Herunter
Project managers: Kwan Kwok Ying (Village Houses), Liu Chang (Community Center), Viola Huang (Landscape)
Area: 4000 square meters
Commission date: April 2012
Images: Rural Urban Framework
Donor: Nan Fung Group

Site plan

Jintai Village is located near Guangyuan, Sichuan Province, one of the places hardest hit by the Wenchuan earthquake on 12 May 2008. The disaster left nearly five million people homeless and it is estimated that 80 percent of all buildings in the affected area were destroyed. Over the past five years, major reconstruction efforts have taken place. However, in July 2011, after heavy rainfall and landslides in the region around Jintai Village, several newly rebuilt homes and houses under construction were destroyed once more. Despite the occurrence of this later tragic event, locals did not receive further donations or aid. Supported by the local government and NGOs, this project demonstrates a socially and environmentally sustainable model for earthquake reconstruction while examining the many nuances involved in reconstructing a local community.

A total of 22 houses will be rebuilt, including a community center. The design strategy provides four types of houses differentiated by their roof sections. These structures will demonstrate new uses for local materials, biogas technologies, accommodations for pigs and chickens, and green, stepped roofs. A vertical courtyard improves lighting and ventilation and channels rainwater for collection. The design also promotes reed bed waste-water treatment and collective animal rearing. By linking various village programs to the ecological cycle, environmental responsiveness is heightened, transforming the village into a model for surrounding regions. Notably, the proximity of units encourages village interdependency in addition to porosity, as ground spaces are shared by the community.

This is an investigation into modern rural livelihood. Villages are generally understood to be naturally evolving places and hometowns, so a planned village is odd compared to a planned city. With tens of thousands of newly planned villages occurring in China today, the challenge is to reassert the village as an ontological ideal—to plan villages as authentic places where spatial organization and physical expression is derived directly from the village's relationship to its natural environment.

Village aerial view

Roofscape

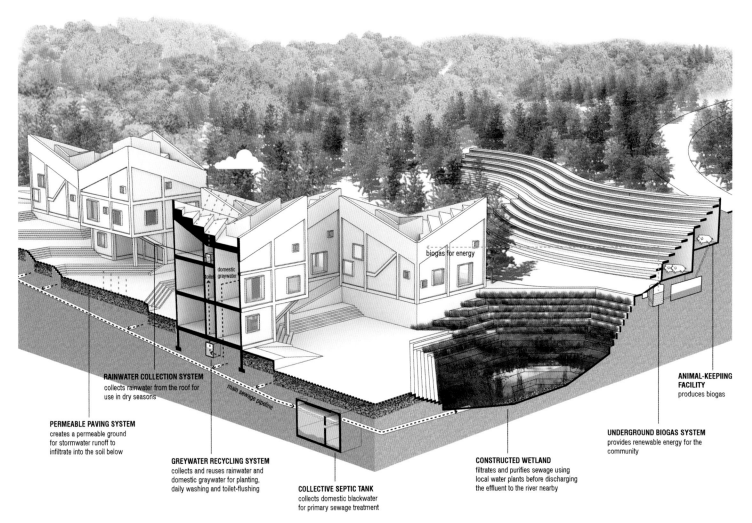

RAINWATER COLLECTION SYSTEM
collects rainwater from the roof for
use in dry seasons

biogas for energy

domestic
graywater

main sewage pipeline

**ANIMAL-KEEPIING
FACILITY**
produces biogas

PERMEABLE PAVING SYSTEM
creates a permeable ground
for stormwater runoff to
infiltrate into the soil below

GREYWATER RECYCLING SYSTEM
collects and reuses rainwater and
domestic graywater for planting,
daily washing and toilet-flushing

COLLECTIVE SEPTIC TANK
collects domestic blackwater
for primary sewage treatment

CONSTRUCTED WETLAND
filtrates and purifies sewage using
local water plants before discharging
the effluent to the river nearby

UNDERGROUND BIOGAS SYSTEM
provides renewable energy for the
community

Ecosystem diagram

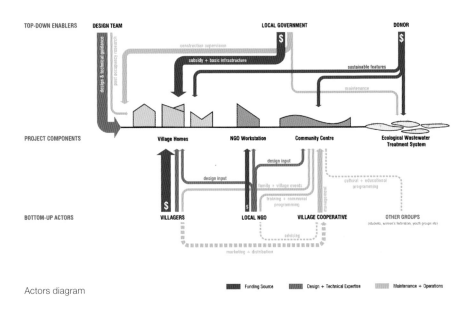

TOP-DOWN ENABLERS   **DESIGN TEAM**   **LOCAL GOVERNMENT**   **DONOR**

construction supervision

design & technical guidance
post occupancy research

subsidy + basic infrastructure

sustainable features

maintenance

PROJECT COMPONENTS

Village Homes   NGO Workstation   Community Centre   Ecological Wastewater
                                                        Treatment System

design input

design input

family + village events

cultural + educational
programming

training + communal
programming

BOTTOM-UP ACTORS   **VILLAGERS**   **LOCAL NGO**   **VILLAGE COOPERATIVE**   **OTHER GROUPS**
                                                                                (students, women's federation, youth groups etc)

advising

marketing + distribution

Actors diagram

Funding Source   Design + Technical Expertise   Maintenance + Operations

A villager working on the green stepped roof

Model

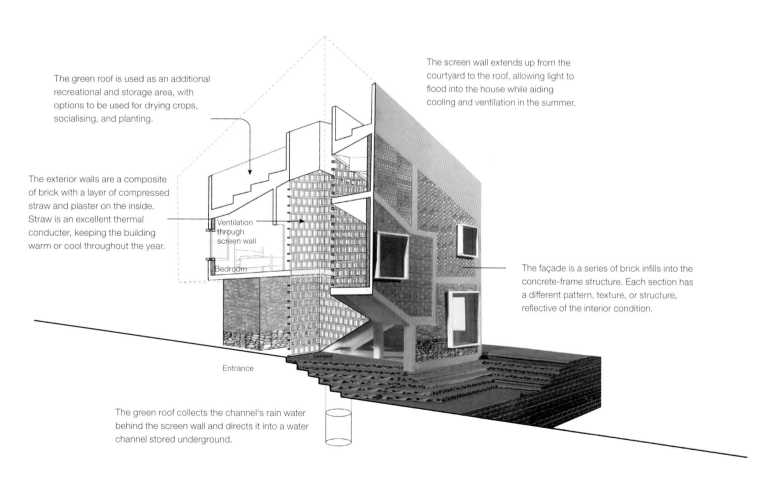

The green roof is used as an additional recreational and storage area, with options to be used for drying crops, socialising, and planting.

The screen wall extends up from the courtyard to the roof, allowing light to flood into the house while aiding cooling and ventilation in the summer.

The exterior walls are a composite of brick with a layer of compressed straw and plaster on the inside. Straw is an excellent thermal conducter, keeping the building warm or cool throughout the year.

Ventilation through screen wall

Bedroom

The façade is a series of brick infills into the concrete-frame structure. Each section has a different pattern, texture, or structure, reflective of the interior condition.

Entrance

Courtyard

The green roof collects the channel's rain water behind the screen wall and directs it into a water channel stored underground.

House section diagram

YANGLIU VILLAGE RECONSTRUCTION

Hsieh Ying-Chun | Hsieh Ying-Chun Architects

Location: Mao County, Sichuan, China
Architect: Hsieh Ying-Chun Architects & Design for People Co., Ltd.
Structure: Reinforced light-gauge steel frame, stone, wood, coated-steel roof plate
Design and construction period: September 2008–September 2009
Area: 27,439 square meters (site); 11,723 square meters (floor area); 67 square meters (house; 56 houses)

Site plan

Yangliu Village is one of the few Qiang tribal minority villages that still maintains its Qiang cultural and linguistic traditions. After the devastating earthquake on 12 May 2008, architect Hsieh Ying-Chun gathered his team on-site and assembled the returned local villagers to discuss the reconstruction of their homes. With mutual aid and labor-sharing methods among the villagers, reconstruction of 56 houses was successfully completed within one year.

The Qiang are mountain dwellers skilled in construction. They build homes on the rockiest cliffs and beside the swiftest rivers. Also, renowned stonemasons, they live in granite-stone houses generally consisting of two to three stories. With these traditions and local craftsmanship heritage in mind, the design of the new homes was based on the vernacular Qiang fortress. The first floor is used to keep livestock and poultry, the second floor is the living quarters, and the third floor is for grain storage. Exterior corridors of each house are connected to create an exchange space.

Light-gauge steel frames were implemented in the beginning of the reconstruction process. Work began from a basic 'open' structural layout, giving individual families a great deal of freedom to adjust plans according to their circumstances and needs. As the village lies deep in a mountain valley with restricted access to modern machinery, construction was completed solely by manpower. Similar to the traditional Qiang building process of timber framing, villagers erected steel structures of the houses by hand, accompanied with traditional Qiang folk songs and the confidence achieved from past experiences.

In these deficient and extreme circumstances, the abundant knowledge and experience of local building methodologies become apparent. The open framework of the design, allows the combination of local building materials and craftsmanship to fully express its potential. Rubble was salvaged and reused as infill for bottom exterior walls. Minimal concrete was used to build second-story walls. Recycled timber from formwork was used for third-story walls.

The simplified construction process using these frameworks allows all villagers, regardless of age, gender, or profession, to fully participate in the process of rebuilding their own houses. The light-gauge steel open framework is a building technology that not only promises a structurally safe environment for dwellings, but also a resilient methodology that addresses the abundant social and cultural values inherent in the discipline of architecture.

Construction process

Village aerial view

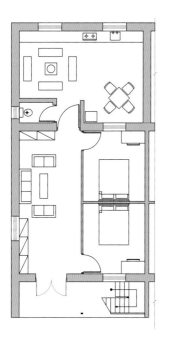

First-floor plan

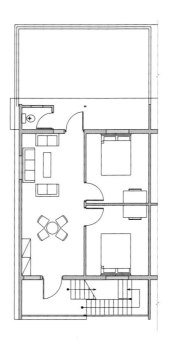

Second-floor plan

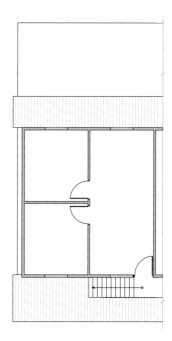

Third-floor plan

Longitude elevation

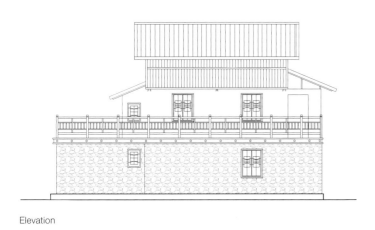

Elevation

Section

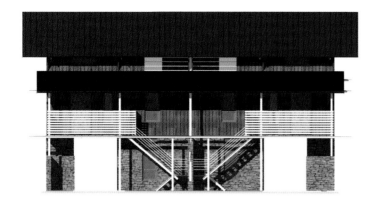
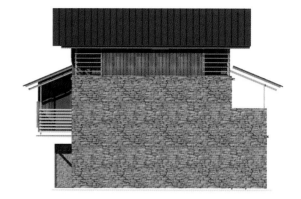

Photo-collaged elevations

Construction process

PRODUC

TION

The ongoing rural development is unprecedented in terms of economic capital, social motive, and technological condition. With its labor backflow and the diversification of production, the countryside is also a focus for national policy. The transformation from a rural society to a market society is drastic: various industries settle in there, infrastructure updates, production and consumption systems also matures. In order to meet production needs, architecture in the countryside also adapts and adjusts, which is manifested in its built environment and social forms.

Production

Zhang Lei creates an astonishing interior space for **Wood Kiln Bingding** to raise more awareness from local government and offer new opportunities to the ancient craft of porcelain-making. The rituality of the linear space of the kiln is strengthened in the slice installation of the woodkiln chamber. Chen Haoru's **Taiyang Organic Farming Commune** and Li Yikao's **Huateng Hog House Exhibition Hall** are both related to the traditional livestock-keeping function of the countryside and seek new possibilities through architectural intervention. Taiyang Organic Farming Commune uses bam-boo and local crafts to construct several simple yet elegant structures for raising livestock. Huateng Hog House Exhibition Hall introduces a water-recycling system in which pig waste is treated and purified to be a waterscape feature for the exhibition hall. In **Wuyishan Bamboo Raft Factory**, Hua Li designs an in-situ concrete structure for the making of bamboo rafts. The austerity and simplicity of the building corresponds to its industrial nature and expresses a strong tectonic capacity. While production is about making, it could also be a place of performance. Xu Tiantian's **Songyang Zhangxi Brown Sugar Workshop** is a stage set for the production of brown sugar with its stress on visual openness and its engagement with tourist experience. The five projects indicate that to preserve the tradition, something new is needed.

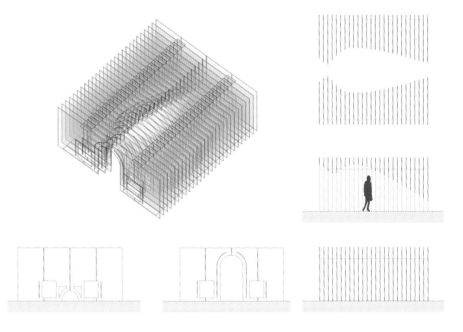

Wood Klin Bingding installation drawings

WOOD KILN BINGDING: SLICES OF THE TRADITIONAL WOOD KILN CHAMBER

Architect: Zhang Lei
Design team: Ma Haiyi, Jin Haibo, Zhang Xue
Material: MDF

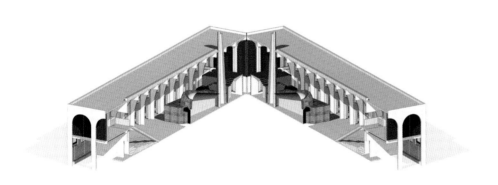

Wood Kiln Bingding model

Wood Kiln Bingding construction process

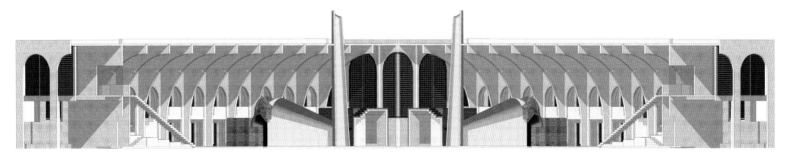

Section of the traditional wood kiln chamber

WOOD KILN BINGDING

Zhang Lei | AZL Architects

Location: Qiancheng Village, Jingdezhen, Jiangxi
Design team: Zhang Lei, Zhang Xue
Area: 3300 square meters (site); 1200 square meters (building)
Design and construction period: 2017–2018

Site plan

The wood kilns of Jingdezhen in Jiangxi, China, are symbols of the traditional industry of porcelain-making, which can be traced back more than 2000 years. Like any other historic handicraft with a long story, the traditional porcelain-making industry has been hit by the technology explosion. Whether the advanced gas kilns offer a better quality of porcelains remains controversial, wood kilns are indeed less efficient and consume more energy and time. Due to the widespread use of industrial fuels such as coal and natural gas and the higher environmental requirement, the wood kilns are facing extinction and the fine tradition is fading away.

The owner of Wood Kiln Bingding, Mr. Yu, with a background in modern engineering, is also a practitioner who shows great interest in revitalizing the tradition. As a successor to the kiln-construction and porcelain-making master, Mr. Yu knows not only how to build a traditional wood kiln but also how to use it to make fine porcelain. That is quite rare in Jingdezhen as today only four people know how to do it in the authentic way.

The architecture of Wood Kiln Bingding is the kiln itself. The chamber takes about a quarter of the space and is entirely built by Mr. Yu and his master following Luanyao, a traditional method of kiln construction. The fair-faced concrete kiln is the shelter of the chamber. While meeting the spatial requirement of the porcelain-making process of loading, firing, and drawing, the concrete kiln magnifies the experience of visiting the place, making sure that porcelain artists, collectors, and visitors can participate in the whole process. Today, the construction of wood kilns is a respectable handicraft and the entire porcelain-making process is a ritual to show great respect and awe to our fine traditions.

Wood Kiln Bingding is located in Qiancheng Village of Jingdezhen. In this beautiful and peaceful hilly village, Mr. and Mrs. Yu and the local government are trying to revive the wood kilns in the hope of bringing more attention to the local porcelain industry and offering new opportunities to traditional craftsmanship and economic development. After all, in Chinese culture, porcelain has never been taken simply as a necessity of our daily life, rather it is more of a medium through which we experience and taste life.

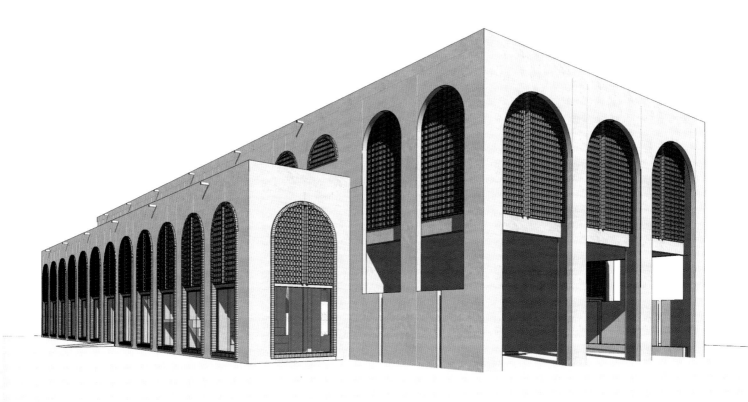

Wood Kiln Bingding exterior view

1 | 2
   | 3

1. Gallery view
2. View of the axis space
3. View of the wood kiln chamber

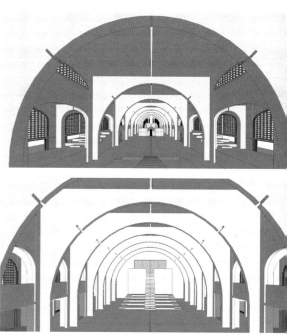

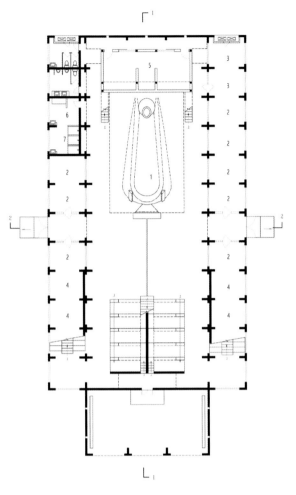

First-floor plan

1. Kiln
2. Infill area
3. Grinding area
4. Storage
5. Foyer
6. Locker room
7. Bathroom
8. VIP room
9. Exhibition area

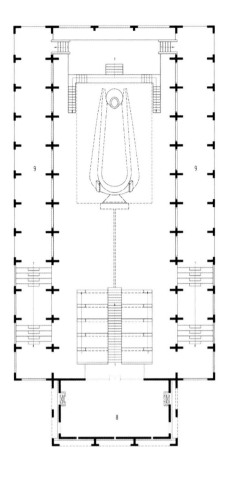

Second-floor plan

0 2 4 10m

0 2 4 10m

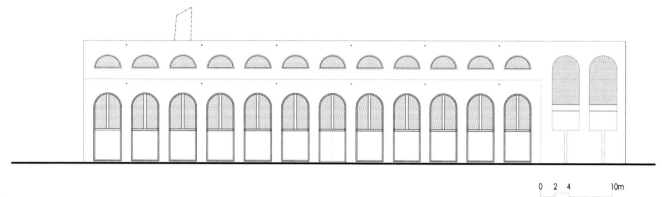

West elevation

0 2 4 10m

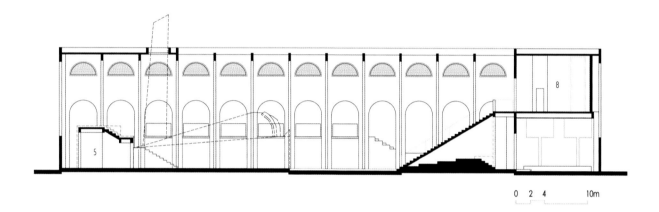

Section 1-1

0 2 4 10m

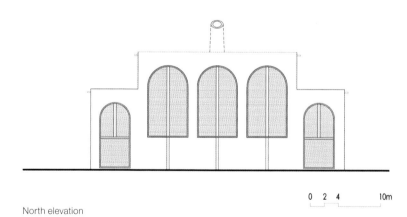

North elevation

0 2 4 10m

1. Kiln
2. Infill area
3. Grinding area
4. Storage
5. Foyer
6. Locker room
7. Bathroom
8. VIP room
9. Exhibition area

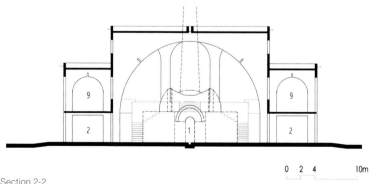

Section 2-2

0 2 4 10m

TAIYANG ORGANIC FARMING COMMUNE

Chen Haoru | Atelier Chen Haoru

Location: Lin'an
Architect: Atelier Chen Haoru
Design team: Chen Haoru, Xie Chenyun, Ma Chenglong, Wang Chunwei, Zhu Xiaocheng, Gu Anjie
Structure: Bamboo, thatch, stone
Area: 2000 square meters (pigsty site); 256 square meters (pigsty); 130 square meters (henhouse)
Design and construction period: 2013–2014
Photography: Heng Zhong

Site plan

This project was conducted in a village with 140 farming households located in the mountainous region west of Hangzhou. The primary material used for construction was local bamboo and pebbles from nearby streams. One craftsman, Mr. Chen, was the eldest son of a local farmer. Local workers and materials were used for all aspects.

In the first part of the design process, animal behavior was studied while rotational grazing methods and the feeding-ground arrangement were planned out. The pigsty was designed with areas for sleeping and feeding, an outdoor toilet, an open-air field, and a pool. No additional excavation was required for the site; instead, a stable structure was constructed from enormous bamboo stems.

The commune organized villagers to knit together thatch picked from the nearby mountains, which workers then hung onto the roof of the bamboo structure.

The henhouse was built on a patch of compacted flat earth located between the small agricultural reservoirs at the end of the valley and the hills to the north. A shallow foundation was formed by inserting small wooden stakes into the ground in a uniform pattern. A platform was constructed from bamboo on top of this foundation. Two 8-by-8-meter bamboo structures were placed on top of this platform, forming an open and sturdy structure. A simple, quickly constructed roof of bamboo tiles was added to the top of the structure, giving it additional stability. The interior is tall and roomy, containing a dense arrangement of poles, on which birds can alight.

While thatch can only be harvested in certain seasons, bamboo is readily found throughout the region. For this reason, bamboo tiles were chosen for the roof structure. Each bamboo stem was split into two pieces, forming two arc-shaped halves that function as natural tiles. After drilling holes through the joints of the bamboo, these halves are ideal for lining up as roof tiles. Craftsmen clean out each joint with hammers to ensure that the front and back faces fit together. In total, more than 200 bamboo stems were used in the roof structure, with no chemical waterproofing necessary.

Overall view of the pigsty

Henhouse by the water

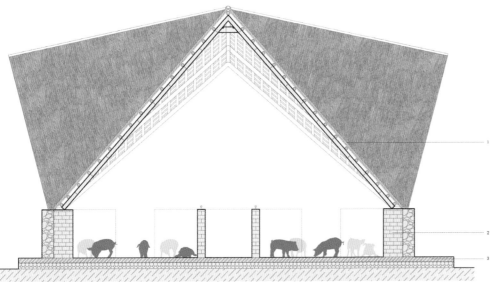

Section A-A of pigsty

1. 50 mm thatch
   20 mm bamboo chips
   Φ100 mm bamboo sticks
   Φ100 mm bamboo bearer
2. 300 mm cobble wall
   500 mm brick wall
3. 20 mm cement plaster to falls (2 percent)
   120 mm light brick floor
   150 mm precast hollow concrete plank
   Compacted soils

Pigsty interior view

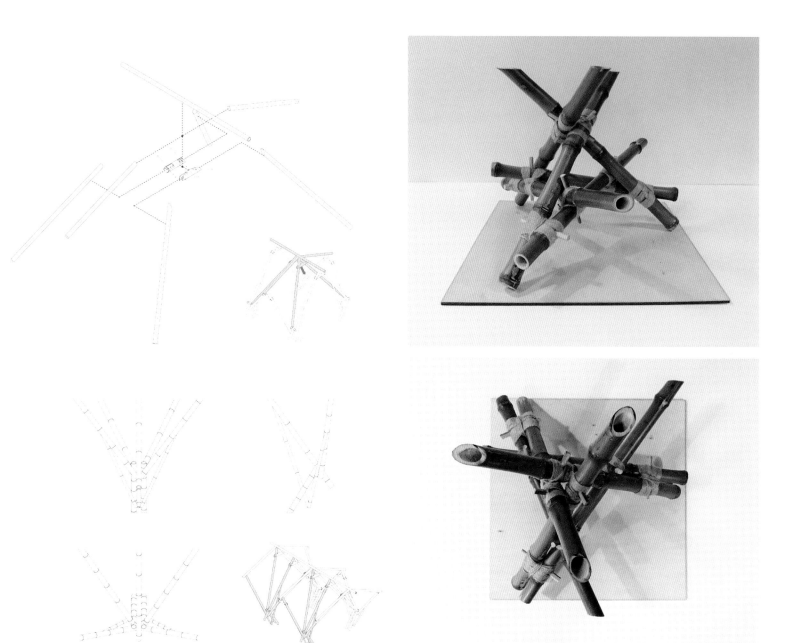

Bamboo structure details and model

Long pavilion elevation

HUATENG HOG HOUSE EXHIBITION HALL

Li Yikao | Leeko Studio

Location: Huateng Ranch, Zhouquan County, Tong Xiang, Zhejiang Province
Architect: Leeko Studio
Team: Li Yikao Jiadianxin
Area: 1500 square meters
Project completion: 2016
Photography: Zhang Yong

Site plan

Huateng Hog House Exhibition Hall in Tongxiang, Zhejiang, was Leeko Studio's first rural construction project. The Huateng Animal Husbandry ranch desired a building to display its pork processing and pork products, and to serve as a starting point for further tourism development projects. Leeko Studio's design incorporated a combination of red brick, concrete, washed stone, natural light, and water, as well as improvisation by workers.

This project required Leeko Studio to attempt a new type of design. With what type of attitude should an architect confront China's current large-scale rural construction? How can designs be created easily? How, in locations with insufficient architectural craftsmanship support, does one achieve the ideal of "rough on the outside but fine on the inside"? How can one construct buildings in a more relaxed and natural way?

Before designing the exhibition hall, we first renovated the façade of the pigsty. This was merely a prelude, through which we came to know the form of the pigsty and gained a rudimentary understanding of Huateng's high-tech hog-raising methods. This basic knowledge inspired us to create an architectural form for the exhibition hall that was an evolution of the basic architectural form of the pigsty. The exhibition hall retains the original pigsty profile, with the addition of a light tube to provide natural light and ventilation. At the time, it was believed that daylighting was the building's only chance for success. Due to budgetary reasons, work on the skylight was not begun, but existing natural light was retained.

At the start of the project, the owner introduced us to the company's high-tech hog-raising methods. Belgian experts have been invited to help guide pig-farm construction and feed research. A management system is employed to monitor the health of pigs, isolate sick pigs, and ensure that pigs do not require antibiotic treatments. Out of the many advanced technologies used on the ranch, the only one applicable for display in the exhibition hall was the water recycling system. Ordinary pig farms discharge pig manure directly into the environment, creating pollution. At the Huateng ranch, pig manure is extracted, dried, carbonized, and converted to high-quality fertilizer that can be sold for a relatively high price. Pig urine and rinse water from the pigsty is sent to a series of purification ponds. These ponds contain a variety of plants arranged according to their specific water treatment capacities. After purification, the water is diverted to the exhibition hall, where it appears as a scenic feature between the exhibition hall and the gallery.

Huangteng Hog House Exhibition Hall entrance

Waterscape in the exhibition hall

Skylight

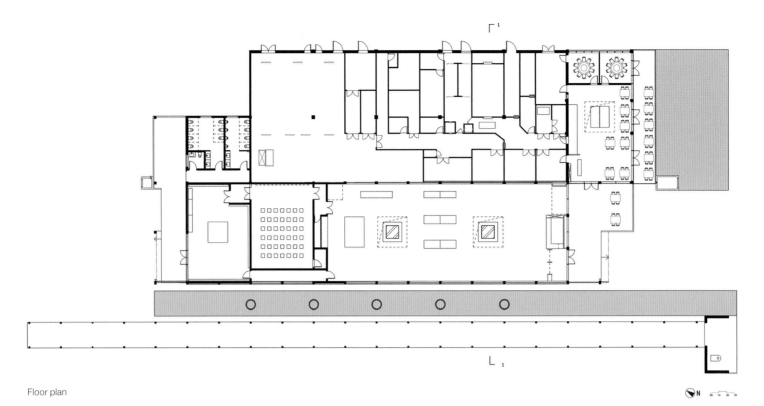

Floor plan

Elevation

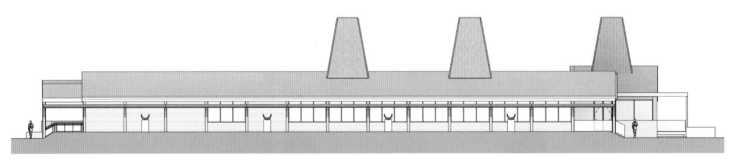

Section 1-1

Corridor night view

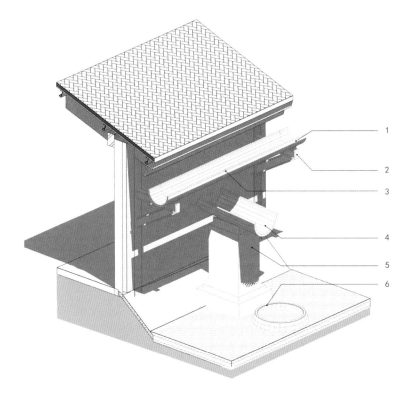

Waterscape detail

1. Water pipe (DN600 glass steel pipe)
2. Steel plate
3. Drain gully, 150 X 150 mm
4. Water pipe (DN800 glass steel pipe)
5. Base with rose-stone finishing
6. Water vat

WUYISHAN BAMBOO RAFT FACTORY

Hua Li | Trace Architecture Office

Location: Xingcun Town, Wuyishan Mountain, Fujian, China
Architect: Hua Li / Trace Architecture Office (TAO)
Design team: Hua Li, Elisabet Aguilar Palau, Zhang Jie, Laijing Zhu, Lai Erxun, Martino Aviles, Jiang Nan, Shi Weiwen, Lian Junqin
Structure: In-situ concrete, hollow concrete blocks, cement tile, bamboo, wood
Design period: 2011–2012
Construction period: 2012–2013 (workshop, office, dormitory; storage unbuilt)
Area: 14,629 square meters (site); 16,000 square meters (workshop: 1519 square meters; office and dormitory: 1059 square meters)
Photography: Su Shengliang

Site plan

Located atop a plateau in the rural Xingcun village, this building complex is a manufacturing and storage facility for bamboo rafts used for tourist purposes: sailing the nearby Nine Bend River in Wuyi Mountain. Each winter 22,000 bamboo stems are harvested. Following a storage period, these stems are used to manufacture 1800 bamboo rafts annually.

The architecture and layout of the building reflect distinct programmatic, topographical, and climatic requirements. The L-shaped manufacturing workshop accommodates six fire areas for bending bamboo and assembling rafts. The interior of the workshop has an open layout with the 14-meters span required for the working space. Natural light is filtered through oblique skylights that are oriented northward to provide softer and more homogeneous light. In addition to work areas, the workshop houses resting spaces, storage rooms, restrooms, courtyards, and other facilities. The office and dormitory building includes a veranda, with offices occupying the first floor, and the dormitory and cafeteria occupying the second floor. The veranda is shaded by louvers constructed from bamboo, which also provide well-ventilated insulation.

In accordance with the principles of localization and economy, in-situ concrete was used for the structure, hollow concrete blocks for the exterior wall system, cement tile for the roof, and bamboo and wood for the sunshades, doors, windows, and handrails. Surface finishes were kept moderates, allowing each material to present its own distinct character. The industrial nature of the project discouraged superfluous designs. By using the most basic elements for construction, the structural and material logic of the architecture is naturally revealed. This project reconciles aesthetic simplicity with the economy of means, allowing the architecture to demonstrate its tectonic resolution.

View of space under pitched roof of the big workshop

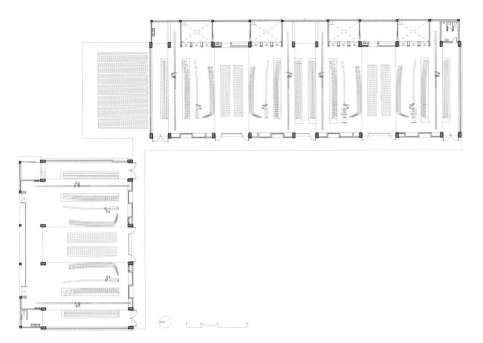

Workshop plan

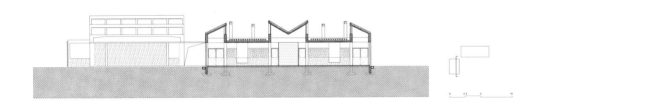

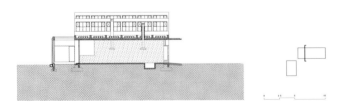
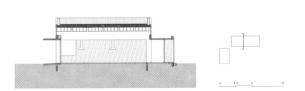

Workshop section

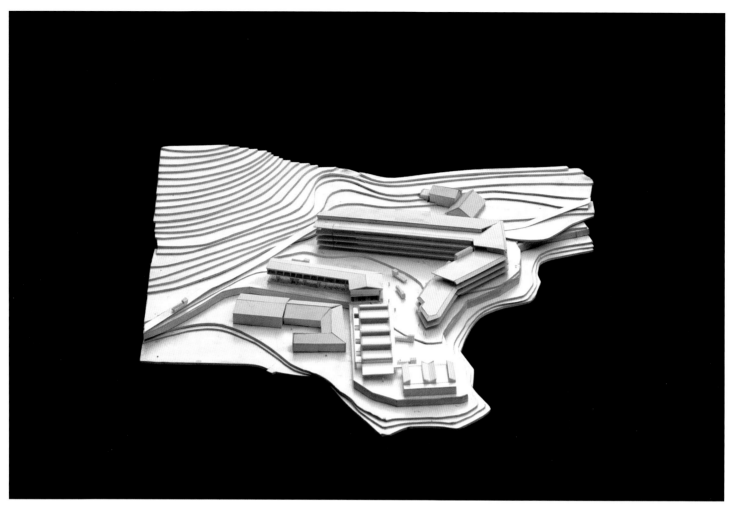

1:500 model

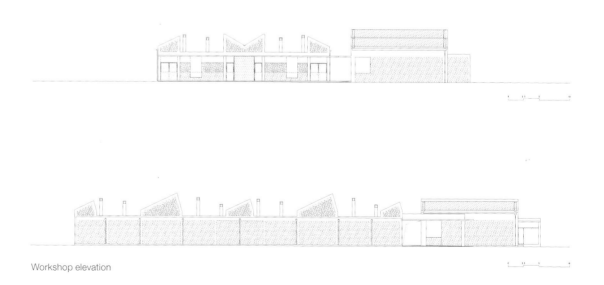

Workshop elevation

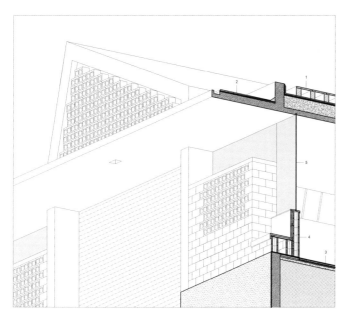

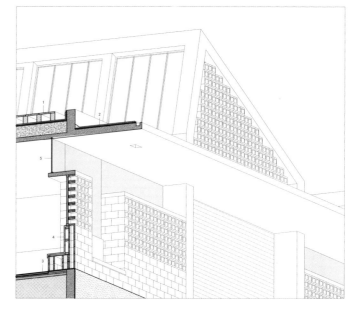

Workshop wall axonometric detail 1

1. 35 mm prefabricated reinforced concrete built on stilts
   190 mm hollow-core concrete brick
   20 mm cement topping
   10 mm separating layer
   4 mm bitumenized roofing felt
   20 mm cement screed
   30 mm 2-percent concrete sloping screed
   Reinforced-concrete roof slab
2. 20 mm cement topping
   10 mm separating layer
   2 mm bitumenized felt
   20 mm cement screed
   Reinforced-concrete roof slab
3. 15 mm cement mortar
   35 mm fine-aggregate concrete
   2 mm waterproofing coating
   Cement screed
   Concrete ground slab
   Soil
4. 190 mm concrete brick
5. Single toughened glass

Workshop wall axonometric detail 2

1. 35 mm prefabricated reinforced concrete built on stilts
   190 mm hollow-core concrete brick
   20 mm cement topping
   10 mm separating layer
   4 mm bitumenized roofing felt
   20 mm cement screed
   30 mm 2-percent concrete sloping screed
   Reinforced-concrete roof slab
2. 20 mm cement topping
   10 mm separating layer
   2 mm bitumenized felt
   20 mm cement screed
   Reinforced-concrete roof slab
3. 15 mm cement mortar
   35 mm fine-aggregated concrete
   2 mm waterproofing coating
   Cement screed
   Concrete ground slab
   Soil
4. 190 mm concrete brick
5. Single toughened glass

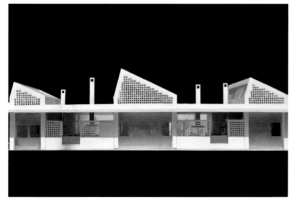

1:50 model of workshop façade

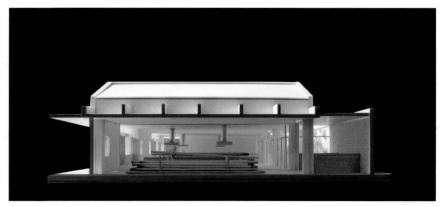

1:50 model of workshop section

1. Interior view of small workshop to the north field
2. Burning area and service wall
3. Interior view of big workshop

SONGYANG ZHANGXI BROWN SUGAR WORKSHOP

Xu Tiantian | DnA Architects

Location: Xing Village, Songyang, Lishui, Zhejiang Province
Architect: DnA Architects
Principal architect: Xu Tiantian
Design team: Xu Tiantian, Zhou Yang,
Lighting design: Zhang Xin Studio, Architecture Department of Tsinghua University
Structure: Steel structure
Area: 1310 square meters (building footprint); 1234 square meters (gross floor area)
Design period: June–December 2015
Construction period: December 2015–August 2016

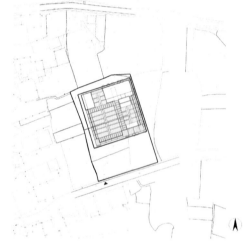

Site plan

Xing Village, Songyang, is a major site for sugar-cane farming and brown sugar production, which are also major income sources for local villagers. As the three remaining workshops were in poor condition, a new facility was in great need.

Our design aimed to encourage villagers' parti-cipation in the production process. Local materials such as bricks and bamboo and an ordinary light-steel structure are incorporated into the project. Programmatically, the brown sugar workshop is both a venue of production and cultural activities. Located where the village extends into a pastoral setting, it offers a beautiful view of the surrounding area for both villagers and tourists.

The production activities inside the workshop are regarded as an everyday performance. With a design that stresses visual openness, the production site is also a performance site. It is a stage for rural production as well as the pastoral environment. Based on four major programs of production, storage, experience, and office, the space is divided into a 田 shape, which is the Chinese character for farmland. The south area is the production zone looking out toward the pastoral surroundings. The north area is an experience zone with a view of trees. By combining production and cultural activities, the project creates a place connecting the village and farmlands.

Courtyard

Exterior view

Brown sugar workshop

View of the courtyard

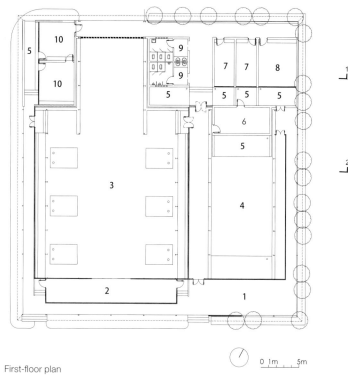

First-floor plan

1. Corridor
2. Drying
3. Working area
4. Exhibition
5. Courtyard
6. Storage
7. Packing
8. Sample showroom
9. Restroom
10. Office

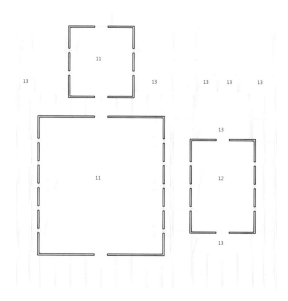

Second-floor plan

11. Working area overhead
12. Exhibition area overhead
13. Courtyard overhead

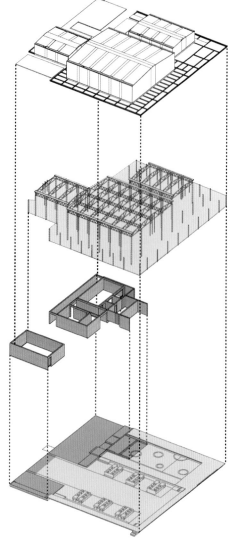

Exploded program and structure diagram

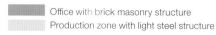

▪ Office with brick masonry structure
▫ Production zone with light steel structure

North elevatoin

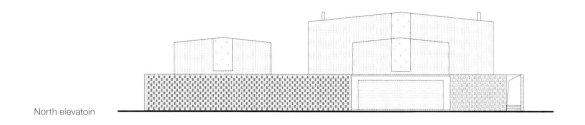

East elevation

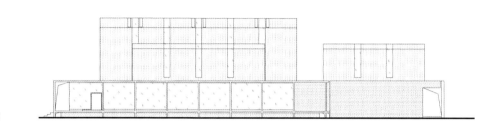

West elevation

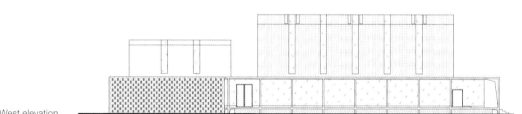

Section 1-1

1. Corridor
2. Working area
3. Exhibition area

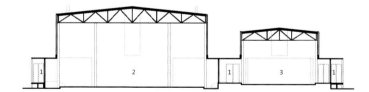

Section 2-2

1. Corridor
2. Working area
3. Office
4. Restroom
5. Packing
6. Sample showing

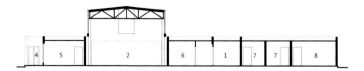

CULTUR

E 文

The countryside is now a testing ground for contemporary art and culture. The avant garde and the vernacular, and the creative and the traditional, meet and result in new sparks. It is not only an expression of culture and a reflection of globalization, but also a revitalization of history and village with artistic and cultural approaches. With memories, cultural events, and the combination of both the old and the new, architects are committed to rural reconstruction not only with architecture's material content and its cultural meanings.

Liu Yuyang creates a station space in his project **Cidi Memo iTown**, responding to the site's context and memory. Inspired by the image of a passing train, as there are several railroads near the building, the station is also a reflection of historical and archetypal models. Similarly, O-office Architects' **Lianzhou Museum of Photography** offers visitors alternating visual experiences between everyday life of the old city and contemporary photographic art. Atelier Archmixing's **Huashu Rural Studio** is also a place of culture in the countryside. Designed as a rural studio, it attracts both locals and booklovers from the city to experience a traditional Chinese lifestyle of reading. Urban

Environment Design Magazine invites a group of internationally renowned architects to creates their vision for the countryside with architecture and culture. Three architects' projects—Li Xinggang, Ryue Nishizawa, and Seung H-Sang—are included here. Together, a camping base service center, a concert hall, and a reception center and other facilities form a cultural infrastructure for the countryside. This is also the focus of Lü Pinjing's **Banwan Village Reconstruction** in which a new rural cultural activity center is added to its existing primary school. The combination of educational and cultural facility enriches rural lives and attempts to regenerate local culture.

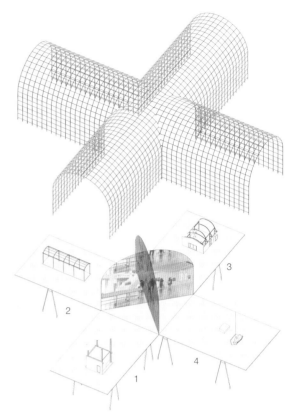

Axonometric exploded diagram

1. Structural module
2. Programmatic module
3. Information module
4. Landscape module

CIDI MEMO, A TOWN OF MEMORY

Design team: Liu yuyang, Lin Yilin, Li Ning, Ji Yuanmei, Lyu Jiajun
Materials: Steel plates and rods, multimedia images and models
Area: 10 square meters (4.8x4.8x2 meters)

Cidi Memo, a Town of Memory is an architectural installation project on the Cidi Memo cultural-creative town. Using 2100 units of steel pinwheel tectonic plates, a 10-square-meter cross-arch structure is created to display a set of four thematic modules: structural, programmatic, landscape, information. Through prototype reconstruction, the installation intends to illustrate a narrative of the space in terms of its accidental birth, random growth, unavoidable demise, and the eventual cultural renaissance.

A land of in-between, the place emerged as a result of several railways cutting through, generating a large amount of low-quality industrial storage spaces that have been subsequently retrofitted and rebuilt into a new cultural-creative town. The upgrades and transformations of these spaces brought an influx of people and businesses, as well as organic and unpredictable changes of lifestyle, creating a new synergy for the community and momentum for growth. Passenger and cargo trains still passing through the site every few minutes vividly reminds us—like a movie scene—of the brevity of history and breath of imagination for this place. In this regard, the meaning and value of architecture is closer to those of a continuously operating transport infrastructure. Architecture becomes a two-way synchronized "cultural infrastructure," providing spaces for cultural production on one hand, and transporting cultural contents, services, and products on the other hand. Since its opening in December, 2016, the curatorial events and operational efforts conducted at Cidi Memo Town have demonstrated a new possibility for the design-driven cultural-creative model that can serve as an exemplary case study for many other future places in China.

CIDI MEMO ITOWN

Liu Yuyang | Atelier Liu Yuyang Architects

Location: Chaoyang District, Beijing
Architect: Atelier Liu Yuyang Architects
Principal architects: Liu Yuyang
Project architect: Li Ning
Design team: Che Peiping, Wu Yaping, Lian Funing, Yang Ke, Che Jin, Luo Kun, Wang Xiaoling
Structural consultant: Shanghai Yuangui Structural Des. Firm Inc.
Lightning consultant: Unolai Design
Structure: Steel structure
Area: 5500 square meters (site); 6300 square meters (building)
Design period: December 2015–June 2016
Construction period: March–December 2016
Photography: Xia Zhi, Zhu Siyu

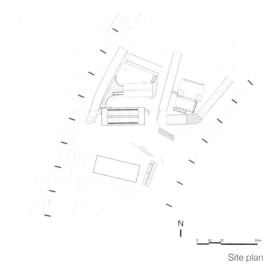

Site plan

The project is located between Beijing's 4th East Ring Road and 5th East Ring Road. Several railroads intersect and divide the site into fragments. We consider the site uncultivated land, isolated, and forgotten while the rest of the urban fabric undergoes rapid development. Primitive vitality is hidden in these broken warehouses, and we saw the potential to create a secret garden in the urban desert.

The site, covering an area of 140,000 square meters, will be revitalized by bringing in cultural and creative industries. As the first party to intervene on this site, we were involved in the building renovation of Startup Block and interior design of the sales office. Startup Block contains three zones: Zone A has a sales office and boutique hotel; Zone B has a mockup office; and Zone C has a restaurant. The total area is 6000 square meters.

One of the greatest challenges of the concept design was tailoring the complex warehouse space to fit its new purpose, as well as increasing overall floor area ratio without altering the building footprint. We connected the warehouses, restructured the spatial organization, and placed public programs at the heart of Startup Block. This strategy brought forward the resulting Station space.

Steel structures offered us greater creative flexibility and naturally became our first choice for the renovation project. The silver, vaulted, carriage-like design was inspired by the image of a passing train. The vault is also a reflection of historical archetypal temples, libraries, and stations. In the sales office, a variant on this vault design houses a floating mezzanine. Curved elements were also applied to façade design as well as door and window details, giving the rough industrial mass a more refined and humane touch.

The composition of the façade is a continuation of the old structure and the new, a contrast between the heavy masonry and the light curtain wall. We used volcanic rock, gray brick, and red brick to underline the heaviness and roughness of the original masonry. On the added volumes, curtain walls with different degrees of translucency, ranging from gray steel sheet and polycarbonate panel to clear glass, were applied.

The Station, an expansion of the sales office space, is reserved for business talks. The name comes from the 9-meter-high western curtain wall that faces the central rail track. A triangular terrazzo bar and a double-sided clock form the centerpiece. The ceiling was finished with backlit corrugated polycarbonate, adorned with a clock and spherical pendant lamps. Inside the Station, as the train passes by occasionally, we are able to imagine a surreal, retro experience.

Cidi Memo iTown next to the railway tracks

1	2
3	4

1. The curved surfaces of station courtyard and the shark-fish gill-shaped window
2. Zone A exhibition hall mezzanine space and the signal tower at a distance
3. Zone A exhibition hall silver acoustic ceiling, along with linear light embellishing the mezzanine
4. The staircase is pure and translucent. Walking inside is like passing through a future world.

Contrast of various materials, including glass curtain wall, red brick, dark-gray steel panel, and sliver corrugated-steel roof

First-floor plan

1. Station
2. Station courtyard
3. Sales center
4. Sales office
5. Meeting room
6. Hotel foyer
7. Hotel courtyard
8. Guest room
9. Facility kitchen
10. Guest room courtyard
11. Commerce
12. Office
13. Restaurant
14. Café

N

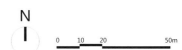

Station space in Zone A

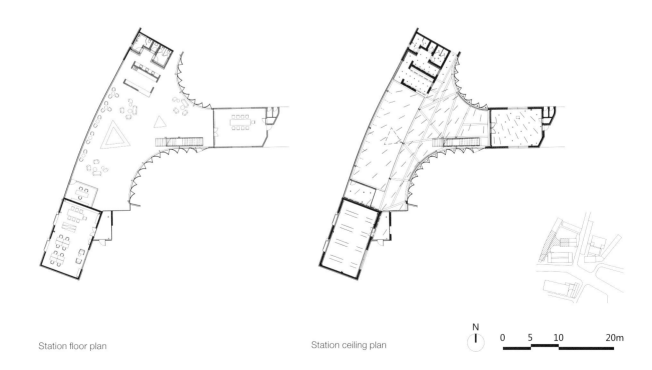

Station floor plan

Station ceiling plan

N

0   5   10   20m

Pure white steel structure and suspended mezzanine in the sales center

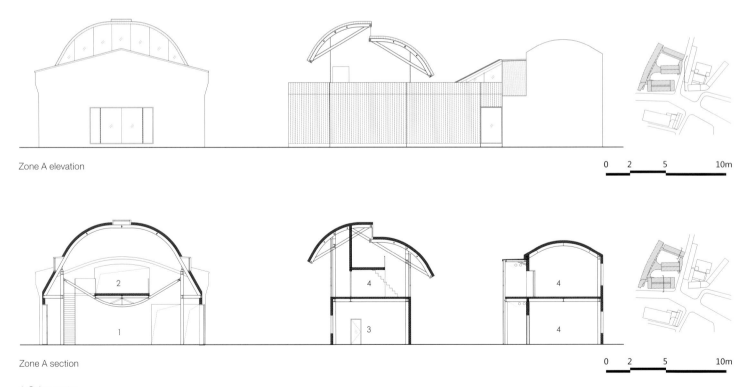

Zone A elevation

0   2   5   10m

Zone A section

0   2   5   10m

1. Sales center
2. Cidi Memo showroom
3. Hotel foyer
4. Guest room

Pedestrian bridge view at upper level at section B

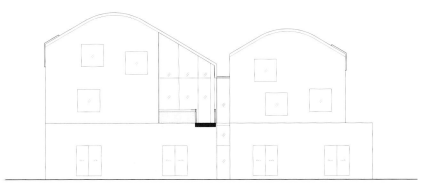

Zone B elevation

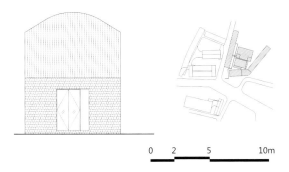

0   2   5   10m

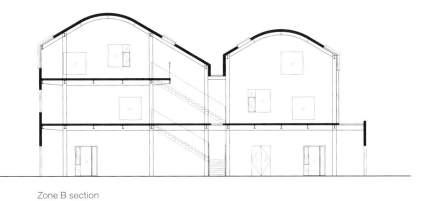

Zone B section

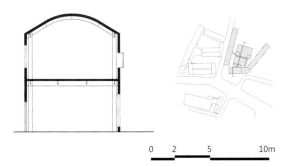

0   2   5   10m

THE ART MUSEUM OF XIAOZUO PENINSULAR AND ITS GARDEN

Dong Yugan | Beijing University of Civil Engineering and Architecture

Location: Xiao Zuo Town, Hui'an County, Quan Zhou City, Fu Jian Province
Architect: Dong Yugan
Design team: Dong Yugan, Du Bo, Zhu Xi
Structure: Steel structure
Area: 5000 square meters
Design period: 1 month
Construction period: 2 months

Site plan

The site is adjacent to a sea, and has no mountains and trees. Before transforming an aban-doned industrial building of the old medicine manufactory of the village into an art museum, I turned the 100-meter-long ridge of the building into a walkway leading toward the sea. This walkway lures people to the café of the museum, which was transformed from an abandoned boiler house. Walking down, one can overlook the sea. The unideal situation of only being able to look afar instead of being able to dwell was ameliorated through turning the nearby filter chambers into a teahouse above a fish pond, sided by a small waterfall.

View of courtyard

View from roof toward courtyard

Roof-ridge passage

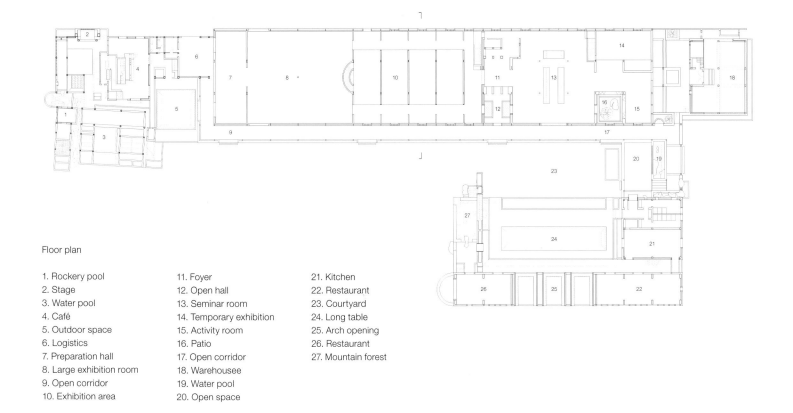

Floor plan

1. Rockery pool
2. Stage
3. Water pool
4. Café
5. Outdoor space
6. Logistics
7. Preparation hall
8. Large exhibition room
9. Open corridor
10. Exhibition area

11. Foyer
12. Open hall
13. Seminar room
14. Temporary exhibition
15. Activity room
16. Patio
17. Open corridor
18. Warehousee
19. Water pool
20. Open space

21. Kitchen
22. Restaurant
23. Courtyard
24. Long table
25. Arch opening
26. Restaurant
27. Mountain forest

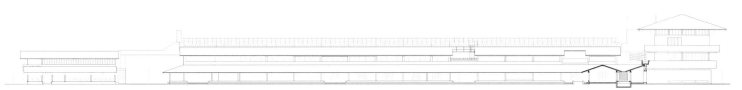

East elevation

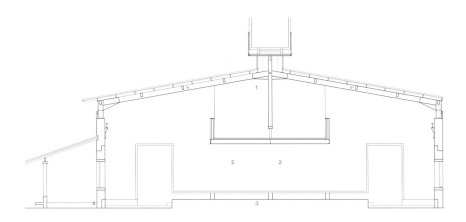

Section

1. Roof-ridge passage
2. Elevated exhibition corridor
3. Exhibition area
4. Open corridor

1. Stair and plants
2. Under the arch

LIANZHOU MUSEUM OF PHOTOGRAPHY

He Jianxing + Jiang Ying | O-office Architects

Location: Lianzhou, China
Architect: O-office Architects
Principal architects: Jianxiang, Jiang Ying
Project architect: Dong Jingyu
Design team: Chen Xiaolin, Lin Licong, Zhang Wanyi, Deng Mincong, Wang Yue, Huang Chengqiang, He Wenkang, Yin Jianjiang, Zeng Ze, Peng Weisen
Structural consultant: Wan Shuqi
Mechanical engineering consultant: Jing Lue M.E. Ltd.
Visual identity design: another design
Area: 3400 square meters
Project completion: December 2017
Photography: Chaos Z, Marco Chen

Site plan

Lianzhou, a small city located in the northern mountain area of Guangdong, has been host to Lianzhou International Photography Festival, one of the most important photographic art events in China, for 13 consecutive years. Construction of the photography museum is considered to have generated the revitalization plan for old downtown. At the same time, the museum is a tribute to the city's past. South Zhongshan Road was chosen as the construction site for Lianzhou Museum of Photography (LMP). Cordially referred to as Old Street by locals, the street is full of traditions and memories. The original site was an old candy warehouse that served as the main venue for the last 12 photo festivals.

LMP is comprised of two interlocking buildings: a preserved, three-story concrete-frame building, and a new U-shaped building constructed on the site of two demolished wooden structures. A composed façade-roof canopy over the new building shapes the roof profile of the museum, fully respecting the urban fabric of the old town. Below the successively folded slopes of the canopy are a series of galleries, interlinked by outdoor corridors, and staircases, with exhibitions and public events taking place under one roof. The existing building and new U-shaped extension create a rich vertical variation inside the building. The U-shaped garden between the two maintains distance and a necessary contrast between the two structures.

The architect has tried to break down the institutional and commemorative tradition of the museum into a three-dimensional exhibition tour that coexists with the old city's morphology. Fragmented scenes from the old city and everyday life are juxtaposed with the experience of a journey of the serious and abstract modern photographic art, but sometimes sarcastic contemporary photographic art. On top of the façade-roof canopy, an open-air theater with a V-shaped section sits directly above the main exhibition hall, connected by a steel terrace cantilevered from the preserved building's flat roof. This piece forms the climax of the entire spatial tour.

Almost all of the construction materials come from local sources. The exterior surface of the continuous façade-roof canopy is composed of gray shingle collected from demolished old houses in nearby urban and rural areas, mixed with a local dark schist (West Bank stone) that was also used on the ground floor and the supporting walls of the basement.

Lianzhou Museum of Photography hiding in Old Street

Various spaces under one roof

Old town and new museum juxtaposed dramatically

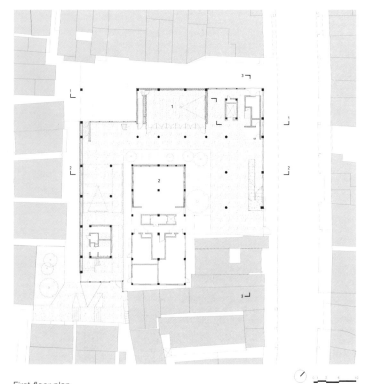

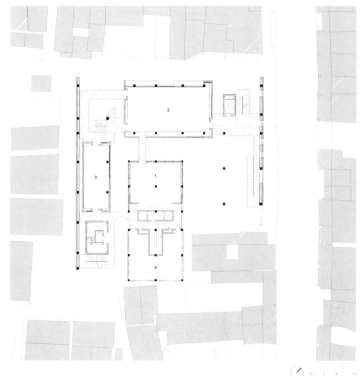

First-floor plan

1. Lecture hall
2. Permanent exhibition hall

Second-floor plan

1. Permanent exhibition hall
2. Main exhibition hall
3. Thematic exhibition hall
4. Storeroom

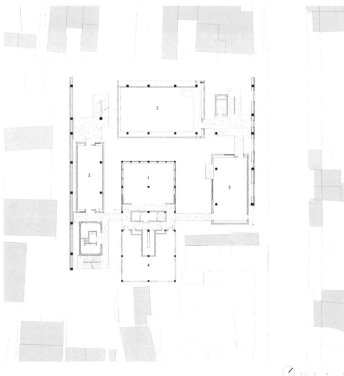

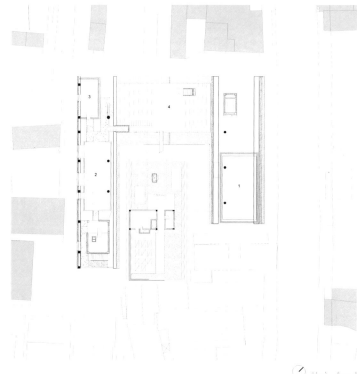

Third-floor plan

1. Permanent exhibition hall
2. Main exhibition hall
3. Thematic exhibition hall
4. Storeroom

Fourth-floor plan

1. Thematic exhibition hall
2. Library
3. Office
4. Rooftoop theater

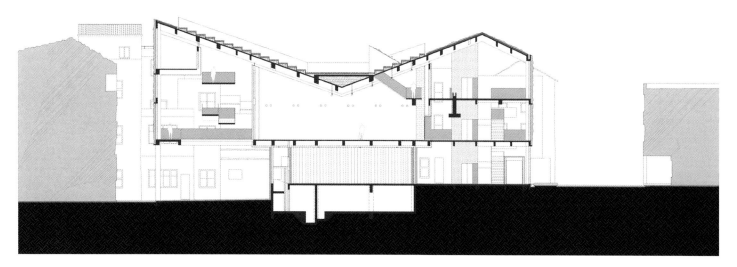

Section 1-1

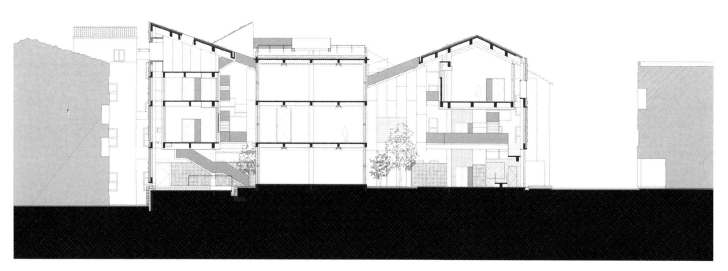

Section 2-2

Lianzhou Museum of Photography

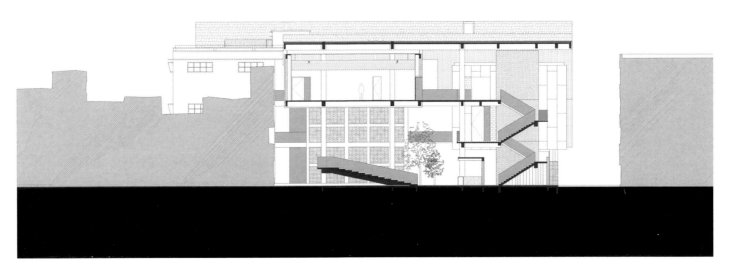

Section 3-3

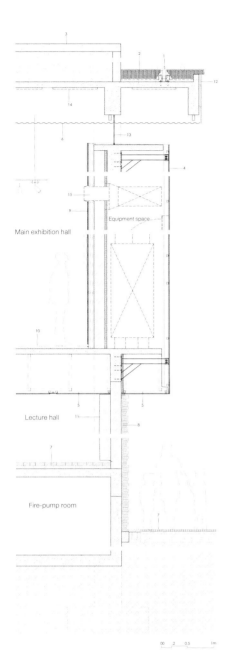

Main exhibition hall

Equipment space

Lecture hall

Fire-pump room

Façade detail 2

1. Local black slate
2. 50 mm irregular local black slate within 15 mm 170x160 mm upright dark-gray tiles
3. Washed granolithic
4. 1.5 mm galvanized steel
5. 1.5 mm galvanized steel gusset plate
6. 1.5 mm anti-UV polycarbonate translucent-white corrugated tile
7. 60 mm irregular local black slate
8. Irregular local black slate stacked
9. 5 mm gypsum plasterboard
10. Hardening cement surface
11. Recycled wooden beams
12. Black-coated steel
13. Fixed casement
14. LED light system inside steel profile
15. Air conditioning

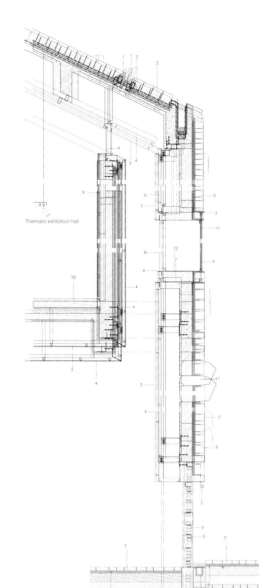

Thematic exhibition hall

Façade detail 1

1. Local black slate
2. 50 mm irregular local black slate within 15 mm 170x160 mm upright dark-gray tiles
3. 50 mm irregular local black slate within 15 mm 170x160 mm upright dark-gray tiles
4. 1.5 mm galvanized steel gusset plate
5. 1.5 mm galvanized steel gusset plate
6. 1.5 mm anti-UV polycarbonate translucent-white corrugated tile
7. 60mm irregular local black slate
8. Recycled wooden windows
9. 5 mm gypsum plasterboard
10. Hardening cement surface
11. Fixed casement
12. Black-coated steel
13. Grass planting tiles
14. LED light system inside steel profile

Aerial view

BANWAN VILLAGE RECONSTRUCTION

Lü Pinjing | Central Academy of Fine Arts

Location: Banwan Village, Yata Town, Ceheng County,
Qianxinan Bouyei and Miao Autonomous Prefecture, Guizhou Province, China
Principal architect: Pinjing Lü
Design team: Qian Cao, Qing Cao, Wei Yang, Tingting Liu, Kangning Zhang,
Ximeng Li, Ce Zhou, Yixin Guo, Chenxi Jia, Changqing Liu, Cheng Liao,
Liqiang Liu
Design and construction period: June 2016–January 2017

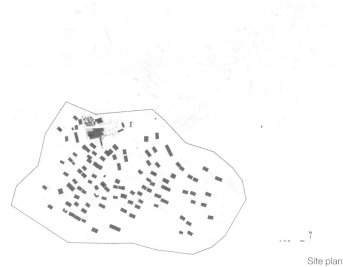

Site plan

The reconstruction of Banwan Village focuses on the preservation of space, the protection, repair, and restoration of traditional settlement morphologies, and the strengthening of rural characteristics. This reconstruction includes: preserving the original condition of a sacrificial space centered around a mountain temple; enriching rural living spaces through the construction of pavilions and the transformation of the canteen; and establishing a rural cultural activity center by improving primary school facilities, reconstructing the village committee building, constructing a new Bouyei cultural education center, stage, and storm bridge, and remodeling pottery kilns. This public space provides an appropriate place for folk activities, ceremonies, festivals, and other events, promotes a harmonious relationship among farmers, and enhances collective consciousness.

The reconstruction emphasizes coordination between new and vernacular buildings. New buildings, which comprise one third of the village's, have a style incompatible with the traditional community. Our design team unified these forms with conventional materials, structures, and crafts, while minimizing the impact on resident families. As for pillar-supported dwellings, which predominate in the village, we strengthened their structures, retained the original method of constructing rammed-earth walls, and repaired vertical wooden paneling based on the unique local style.

Our team transformed one vacant dwelling into an educational site that could serve as a space for the production and teaching of weaving and dyeing crafts. The newly built Bouyei cultural education center, storm bridge, and stage will be used for Bouyei drama performances, seated singing concerts, Bouyei mime shows, and other cultural heritage activities. During the reconstruction of the primary school, we added a "Bouyei heritage and culture classroom" to provide a space for pupils and tourists to learn about Bouyei culture. Remodeling of pottery kilns not only gave new life to traditional pottery crafts, but also created conditions to encourage college graduates from the village to return home and establish businesses. Reconstruction of the brewery provides a good example of a natural balance between protecting traditional crafts and meeting the needs of daily life.

Traditional village reconstruction is a systematic effort, encompassing not only the transformation of buildings and facilities, but also the adaptation and update of rural spatial relations, and utilizing the ingenious strategy of leveraging social exchange to restore relationships. Its goal is the regeneration of rural culture.

Banwan dream primary school aerial view

Banwan village aerial view

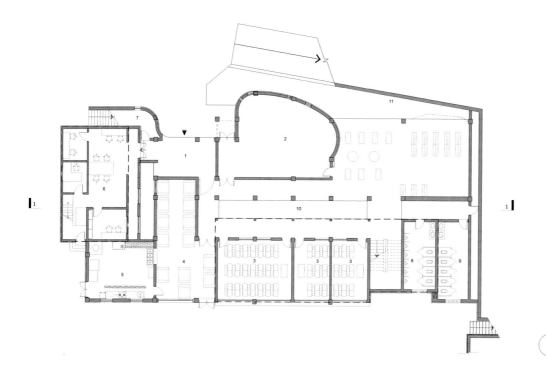

First-floor plan

1. Entrance
2. Ethnic cultural museum
and entertainment classroom
3. Classroom
4. Canteen
5. Kitchen
6. Office
7. Storehouse
8. Men's restroom
9. Women's restroom
10. Gully
11. Paddling pool
☐ Original building

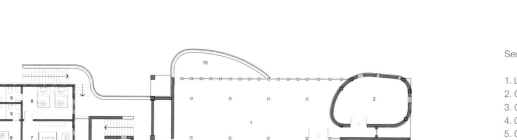

Second-floor plan

1. Library
2. Children's area
3. Office
4. Classroom
5. Corridor
6. Equipment room
7. Living room
8. Dorm room
9. Restroom
10. Roof terrace
11. Outdoor seatings
☐ Original building

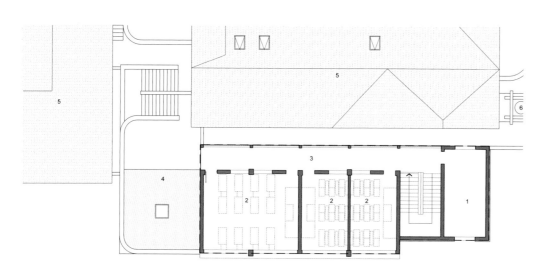

Thrid-floor plan

1. Office
2. Classroom
3. Corridor
4. Roof terrace
5. Roof
6. Structure
☐ Original building

Banwan dream primary school

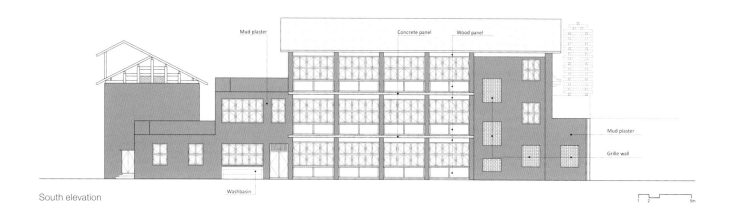

Mud plaster   Concrete panel   Wood panel

Mud plaster

Grille wall

Washbasin

South elevation

1 2   5m

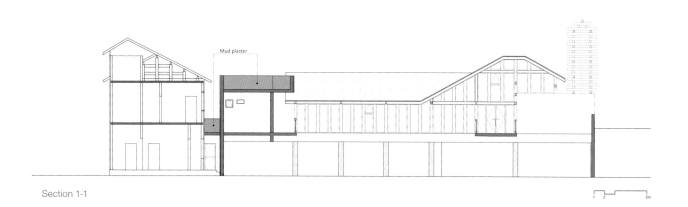

Mud plaster

Section 1-1

1 2   5m

HUASHU RURAL STUDIO

Zhuang Shen + Ren Hao + Tang Yu + Zhu Jie | Atelier Archmixing

Location: Zhouchong Village, Huashu, Nanjing
Architect: Atelier Archmixing/Zhuang Shen, Ren Hao, Tang Yu, Zhu Jie
Design team: Zhuang Shen, Yang Yu, Wang Di, Chen Xiangpeng, Wu Qitao
Structural consultant: Shanghai Wildness Structural Des. Firm Inc.
(General Partnership)
Area: 252 square meters
Design and construction period: 2014–2015

Site plan

Huashu Rural College is located in south of Zhouchong Village, Huashu, Nanjing, at the foot of the dam of Zhouchong Reservoir. The college was renovated from two old rural houses. Designed as a rural studio, the building was later used as a rural library and as the activity room for the village. It attracted booklovers from the city center who wished to experience the traditional Chinese lifestyle of reading when it's rainy and working in the field when it's sunny.

One of the original houses was a barn for rice, the other a farmhouse. The barn had exterior walls built with stones, while the farmhouse had exterior walls built with brick and a surface layer of cement plaster. Nearby villages, faraway factories, high reservoir, and the surrounding farmland, ponds, mountains, and forests form a quiet and serene landscape. The farmhouse had a brighter interior environment, while the barn was darker. The two houses stood side by side at the foot of the dam. The dam was a bit higher than their roofs, allowing visitors to catch a glimpse of the surrounding natural landscape.

The design strategy was one of addition and adjustment. It aimed to discover the characteristics and beauty of the original buildings and their surroundings, and forge unique relationships between them. One focus was reorganization. The bright, brick farmhouse was reorganized into a tidy reading room with an air of formality, while the dark, stone barn was turned into a social space with a quiet atmosphere and rich texture. Another focus was expanding and connecting.

The farmhouse was expanded with the addition of an entrance courtyard and a lofted courtyard. The lofted courtyard offers a view of the surrounding landscape. A long, curved courtyard extending north to the lotus pool was added to the barn as a place for various outdoor acitivies.

View from dam toward studio

Entrance view

Room and beyond

Reading room

First-floor plan

1. Dam
2. Vegetable garden
3. Lotus pool
4. Reading room
5. Social room

N

02   5m

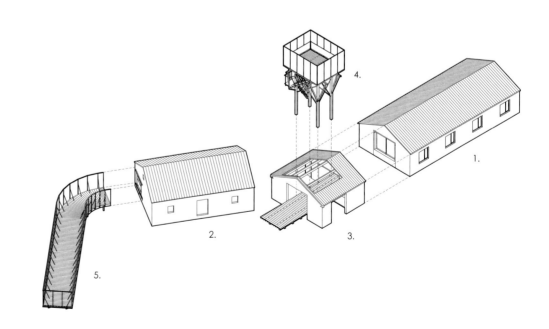

Exploded view of the extension and renovation

1. Reading room
2. Social room
3. Entrance courtyard (addition)
4. Lofted courtyard (addition)
5. Long courtyard (addition)

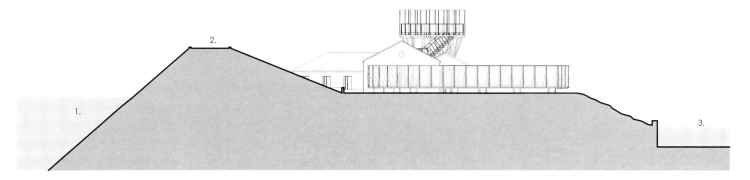

East elevation

1. Tank
2. Dam
3. Lotus pool

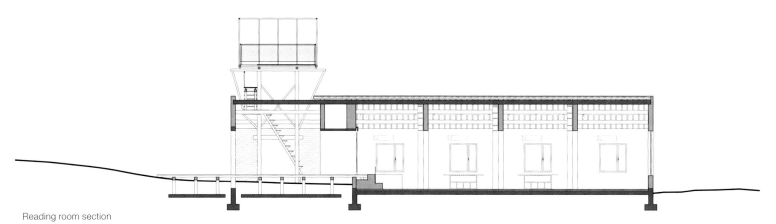

Reading room section

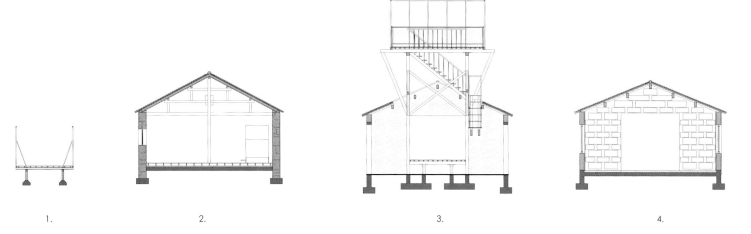

1. Long courtyard section
2. Social room section
3. Entrance courtyard section
4. Reading room section

LOUNA INTERNATIONAL ARCHITECTS' VILLAGE: VILLAGE VISION

Urban Environment Design (UED) Magazine

Against the background of "Beautiful Countryside" and rural revival, China Building Centre (CBC) and Urban Environment Design (UED) Magazine invited internationally renowned architects to visit Louna, and launched Louna International Architects' Village. It aims to build a practical platform for people to explore and output ways of design, construction, and life suited for traditional villages and the future.

Louna is a beautiful village located in Southwest China with unique geological landscapes and the rustic lifestyle of local ethnic minorities. President Xi Jinping has visited Louna and appointed it as one of the pilot regions for the construction of "Beautiful Countryside." Mr. Peng Lixiao, director of CBC and chief editor of UED Magazine, initiated Louna International Architects' Village to realize the transformation of rural construction led by architects through the power of design, culture, art, and media.

Nowadays, Louna has attracted distinguished architects such as Ryue Nishizawa, Seung H-Sang, and Li Xinggang, whose works reveal a rural aesthetics that is rooted in China and led by design and art. Such collective wisdom has been a persuasive evidence to make people believe that architecture can be a shaping force of the formation and logistics of villages by providing a "Village Vision;" that is, to redefine a habitat environment and life quality of Chinese villages in a broad vision. It is predicable that this architects' village is to have a profound influence on the growth patterns of rural areas in China in the future.

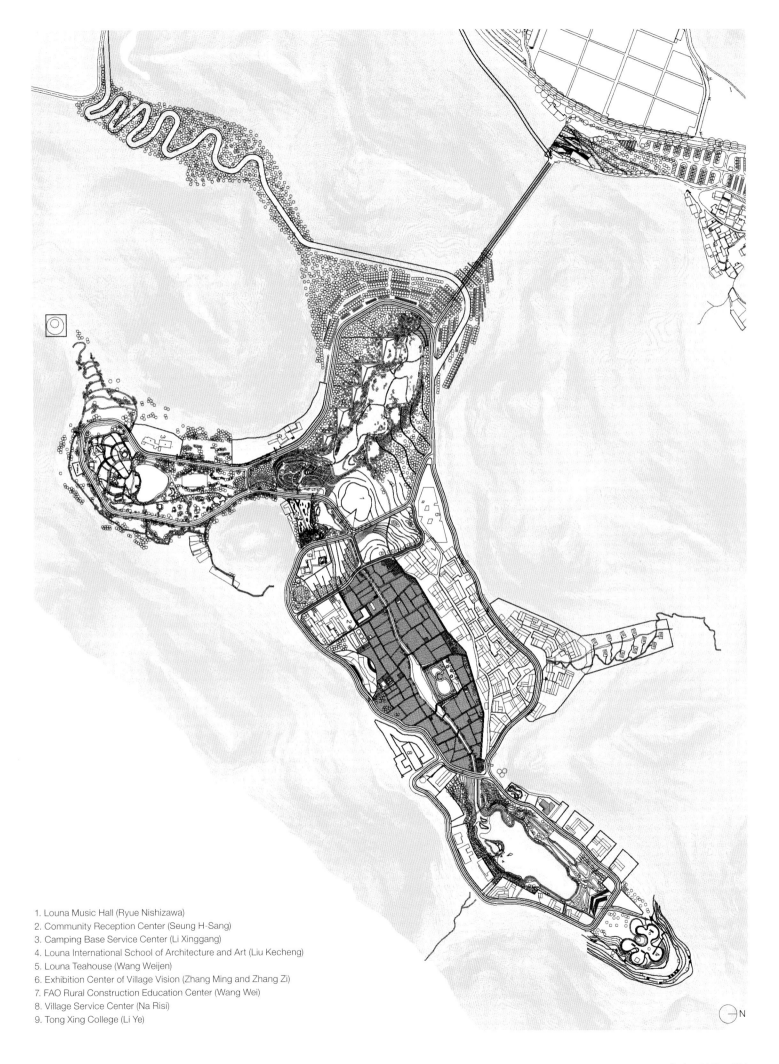

1. Louna Music Hall (Ryue Nishizawa)
2. Community Reception Center (Seung H-Sang)
3. Camping Base Service Center (Li Xinggang)
4. Louna International School of Architecture and Art (Liu Kecheng)
5. Louna Teahouse (Wang Weijen)
6. Exhibition Center of Village Vision (Zhang Ming and Zhang Zi)
7. FAO Rural Construction Education Center (Wang Wei)
8. Village Service Center (Na Risi)
9. Tong Xing College (Li Ye)

N

LOUNA CAMPING BASE SERVICE CENTER

Li Xinggang | Atelier Li Xinggang

Location: Dachong, Louna Village, Xingyi, Guizhou Province
Architect: Atelier Lixinggang
Area: 364 square meters
Design and construction period: December 2016–July 2017; under construction at time of publication

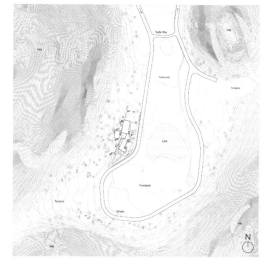

Site plan

Camping Base Service Center is located in southwest Dachong, east of the hills and west of No. 2 Road. The building preserved the outline of original dwellings, with dimensions and materials also kept as design strategies. Local stonemasonry was used to build groups of steps that lead upward to roof level. When seen from a distance, the building appears as a huge rock lying in the hills, melting into the unique landscape of Louna.

According to the foundation of the original dwellings, four traditional courtyards were built for the service center using local methods. Between these are the dining hall, café and reception area, kitchen, conference room and restrooms. Thanks to the close relationship between the rooms and courtyards, when wandering through the structure one can easily sense the different artistic concepts formed by the distant and nearby hills, pond, and tree. The building attempts to bring about an experience where local memories and contemporary tastes can be found. The reception area preserves the spatial typology of traditional local houses, while the restaurant with its cross-shaped column is built like a water pavilion. A corridor connects the courtyards and makes the space flow together. Along the steps near the courtyards, one can step up to the roof platform and enjoy a panoramic view of the beautiful valley.

The building was constructed using a variety of local techniques, such as rubble walls and steps, cross-shaped reinforced-concrete columns, flat roofs and lintels, and prefabricated triangular-corner cement panels. These techniques combine to create a contemporary local space.

Camping Base Service Center courtyard

First-floor plan

1. Outdoor fire
2. Café and reception
3. Courtyard
4. Pond
5. Dining hall
6. Open kitchen

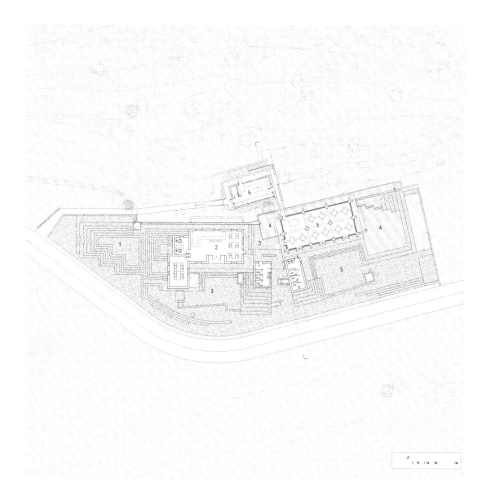

Section

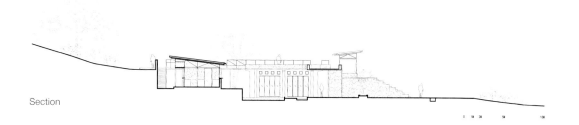

Wall section

1. Polished concrete
2. Mortar leveling layer
3. Concrete cushion
4. Waterproof
5. Mortar leveling layer
6. Foamed-concrete insulation
7. Reinforced-concrete floor
8. Chinese terrazzo
9. Mortar leveling layer
10. Concrete cushion
11. Water
12. Pebblestone
13. Cement leveling layer
14. Reinforced-concrete cushion
15. Rubble steps

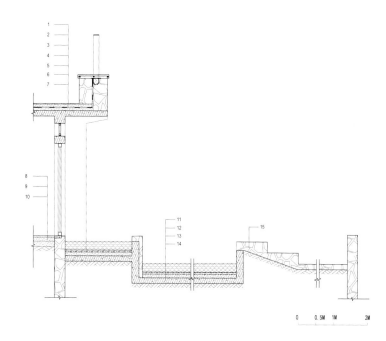

LOUNA MUSIC HALL PROJECT

Ryue Nishizawa | Office of Ryue Nishizawa

Location: Dachong, Louna Village, Xingyi, Guizhou Province
Project team: Ryue Nishizawa, Kenichi Fujisawa, Keita Naito, Masahiro Tachi, Arisa Ueda
Design and construction period: December 2016–July 2017; under construction at time of publication

N

The project is a music hall built in a rural village in Guizhou Province. The site is located at the mouth of a tunnel, which is the entrance to the village. Upon visiting the site, one is impressed by the beautiful mountains surrounding the village and the yellow rapeseed flower fields spreading out into the valley. I thought about a new music hall space where architecture could be fused with the natural environment.

What we proposed is a building with a gentle, unified space made by softly modulating a single large roof. The concrete roof has a freely curved appearance to create various big and small spaces beneath it, separating spaces as it lightly touches the ground, creating openings where it is cut. The roof swells out accordingly where it covers a large and small music hall, whereas the roof is continuous over open spaces such as the foyer and catering area.

A central space in the shape of a shallow basin serves as an outdoor performance area surrounded by architecture and the landscape. As one walks on the undulating roof and enters the building through its openings, this sequence of spaces connecting the inside and outside allows one to experience the space three-dimensionally. Moving from the outside to the inside, from the inside to the outside, over and under the roof, the architecture overlaps two or three layers of space and connects the landscape in a seamless sequence. I thought I could create a concert experience in this beautiful natural location by simultaneously creating a closed space for the music hall and an open space in the landscape. The aim of this new space is to create a landmark for the village and a music hall that responds to the gentle valley and beautiful mountains in which it is built.

Conceptual image

First-floor plan

1. Multifunction room
2. Exterior performance area
3. Entrance hall
4. Catering area
5. Roof terrace
6. Café terrace
7. Small performance hall
8. Large performance hall
9. Make-up room
10. Rehearsal room
11. Artists' terrace

multifunction room · exterior performance area · catering area · interior small performance hall

OH=3356 · OH=3568 · OH=3308

Section A-A

interior large performance hall · lobby · entrance

OH=5322 · OH=3296

Section B-B

catering area · lobby · interior large performance hall

OH=3422 · OH=5600

Section C-C

LOUNA RECEPTION CENTER

Seung H-Sang | IROJE Architects & Planners

Location: Louna, Guizhou Province
Architect: Seung H-Sang
Design team: Lee Dongsoo, Kim Sunghee, Ham Eunah, Kim Bokyeon, An Jinho
Area: 1621 square meters

Site plan

Louna is a village surrounded by mountain terrain and arrived at after passing through a narrow tunnel. It has a gorgeous landscape where small rural houses are grouped among the widespread fields of canola flowers. The reception center stands at the middle of the village. To the south of the center lies a low mountain, and the full view of the village can be seen to the north. To preserve the village's wonderful scenery, the existing houses and small warehouses were redesigned as the new reception center. The center's rooms and spaces are in harmony with the landscape including the canola fields, rural pathways, and small houses. Call it the "Memory of Landscape." The reception center accepted the spatial order and landscript that form the village as is, treasuring the memory of the natural scenery.

The town's rural houses consist of stone-piled walls and a flagstone gable roof. Certain parts of the houses are two stories and one can see the exposed wooden frames inside. This is the traditional and typical form of houses here. The same type of house is used as the entrance hallway of the reception center. Passing the house and a corridor, on the right is a lounge with information desk and an exhibition space renovated from a warehouse. The exhibition provides an introduction of the Louna International Architects' Village. At the south entrance is the restaurant, multi-purpose hall, book café, and guesthouse along the long-spread roofs. The restaurant's façade opens to the outside to provide visitors with a view of the canola fields. Behind the restaurant, lectures and forums can be held in the multipurpose hall for an audience of about 200 people. At the west side of the hall is the

book café, a resting place for multipurpose-hall and guesthouse visitors. The guesthouse is a small facility for maximum nine guests. It faces a mountain to the south, making it a quiet little place to rest.

Each building has a gable roof, just as the farming house, and is arranged along the landscript. The big and small yards between the structures can be used accordingly and they help the visitors enjoy the view of the village. The reception center, which is organized with small houses on a gentle sloped site, might be regarded not just as a single building but as a part of a larger village. The reception center, which will deliver the first impression to the visitors of Louna International Architects' Village, would be a space that not only holds the memories of the town but also opens up a new future.

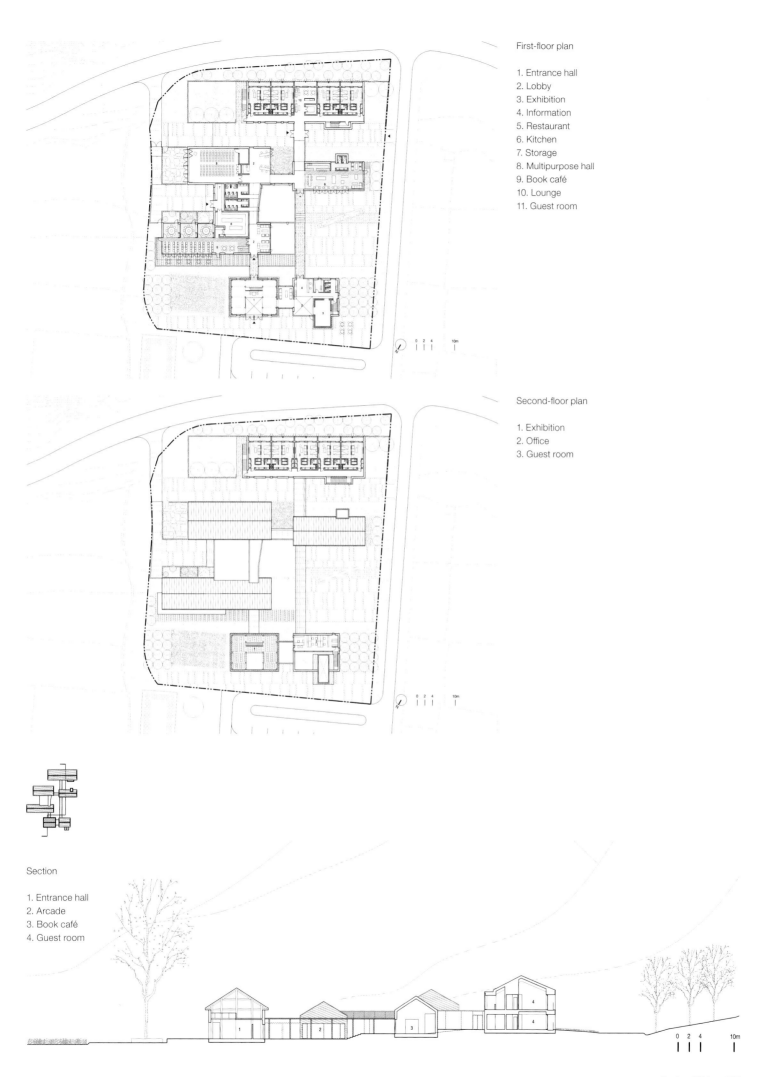

First-floor plan

1. Entrance hall
2. Lobby
3. Exhibition
4. Information
5. Restaurant
6. Kitchen
7. Storage
8. Multipurpose hall
9. Book café
10. Lounge
11. Guest room

Second-floor plan

1. Exhibition
2. Office
3. Guest room

Section

1. Entrance hall
2. Arcade
3. Book café
4. Guest room

ONE VILLAGE, ONE ARCHITECT

RURAL REVITALIZATION PLAN OF LOUNA VILLAGE

Urban Environment Design (UED) Magazine

Location: Louna Village, Yilong New District, Qianxinan Buyei and Miao Autonomous Prefecture, Guizhou Province, China
Sponsors: Yilong District Management Committee, Qianxinan Prefecture, Guizhou Province; Guizhou Louna Architects Commune Cultural Development Co. Ltd.
Supporting media: Urban Environment Design (UED) Magazine
Academic convenor: Kong Yuhang, Deputy Dean, professor and doctoral supervisor of School of Architecture, Tianjin University
Convenor: Peng Lixiao, founder of Louna International Architects' Village, chief editor of Urban Environment Design (UED) Magazine, director of China Building Centre, guest Professor of School of Architecture, Tianjin University
Chief urban planner: Huang Jingtao, president and chief planner of Tianjin Urban Planning and Design Institute, Distinguished Professor of School of Architecture, Tianjin University, recipient of State Council Special Allowance
Chief landscape designer: Xie Xiaoying, principal and chief designer of View Unlimited, Landscape Architecture studio, CUCD, China Urban Construction Design & Research Institute Co.Ltd.
Project period: Commenced October 2017

Design as Rural Catalyst

Rural revitalization is a heated international topic. After World War II, the global economic recovery and the fast rate of urbanization resulted in a lag in the development of rural economies and a widening gap between urban and rural areas. In China, with the urbanization pace slowing, rural revitalization, which has generally become a focus of society, consists of multiple fields and professions, with design being one part of the series plan, albeit a key part and potential catalyst.

Against this background, the rural revitalization plan of One Village, One Architect in Louna, initiated by Louna International Architects' Village, was launched in 2017. The pioneering group of architects, together with universities and colleges jointly invited by the local governments, conducted in-depth consultations for the one-to-one design of villages.

In addition to the design and transformation, attentions would be focused on the construction and development of individual villages. The plan introduced the concept of rural catalyst and promoted work in all areas by drawing upon the experience gained on key points. In addition, the planners, designers, and operators collaborated to consider how to stimulate chain reactions during the village development.

Louna Consensus

The Louna consensus is of: less impact, minimum intervention, delicate design, high-quality and sustainable development, as well as the concept of "transforming the village by designing, restoring the village by arts, guiding the village by culture, and revitalizing the village through industries." It intended to suit the development demand and formulate the plan from the bottom up.

Based on the traditional model of village construction led by the government, Louna Village proposed the bottom-up method. This is based on the actual demand of the village development, guided by the questions that occurred during the village development, and gives priority to the self-built houses of the villagers and their involvement in the process.

The plan is composed of two levels promoted simultaneously. It is intended to establish a bridge for conveying the intentions of villagers and helping resolve problems and formulating the detailed development plan through the village construction plan. It is also intended to integrate the comprehensive development demand so as to establish the objective and strategy based on the regional development planning of the village.

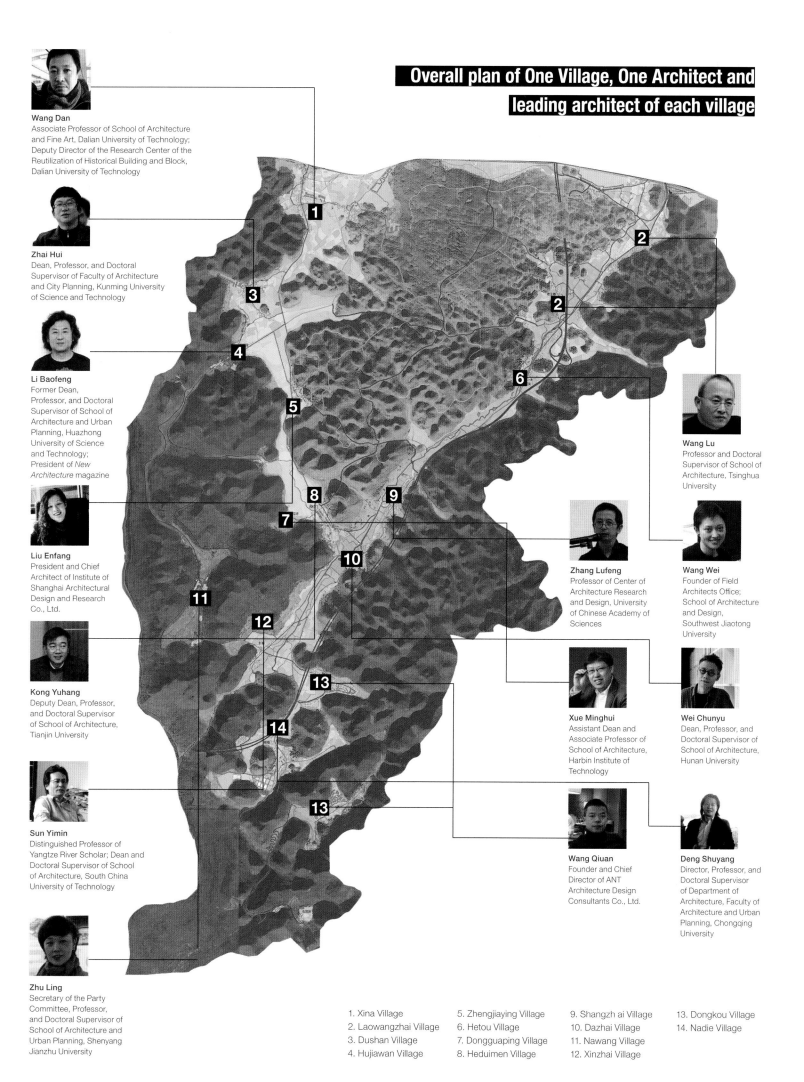

Wang Dan
Associate Professor of School of Architecture and Fine Art, Dalian University of Technology; Deputy Director of the Research Center of the Reutilization of Historical Building and Block, Dalian University of Technology

Zhai Hui
Dean, Professor, and Doctoral Supervisor of Faculty of Architecture and City Planning, Kunming University of Science and Technology

Li Baofeng
Former Dean, Professor, and Doctoral Supervisor of School of Architecture and Urban Planning, Huazhong University of Science and Technology; President of *New Architecture* magazine

Liu Enfang
President and Chief Architect of Institute of Shanghai Architectural Design and Research Co., Ltd.

Kong Yuhang
Deputy Dean, Professor, and Doctoral Supervisor of School of Architecture, Tianjin University

Sun Yimin
Distinguished Professor of Yangtze River Scholar; Dean and Doctoral Supervisor of School of Architecture, South China University of Technology

Zhu Ling
Secretary of the Party Committee, Professor, and Doctoral Supervisor of School of Architecture and Urban Planning, Shenyang Jianzhu University

Wang Lu
Professor and Doctoral Supervisor of School of Architecture, Tsinghua University

Zhang Lufeng
Professor of Center of Architecture Research and Design, University of Chinese Academy of Sciences

Wang Wei
Founder of Field Architects Office; School of Architecture and Design, Southwest Jiaotong University

Xue Minghui
Assistant Dean and Associate Professor of School of Architecture, Harbin Institute of Technology

Wei Chunyu
Dean, Professor, and Doctoral Supervisor of School of Architecture, Hunan University

Wang Qiuan
Founder and Chief Director of ANT Architecture Design Consultants Co., Ltd.

Deng Shuyang
Director, Professor, and Doctoral Supervisor of Department of Architecture, Faculty of Architecture and Urban Planning, Chongqing University

1. Xina Village
2. Laowangzhai Village
3. Dushan Village
4. Hujiawan Village

5. Zhengjiaying Village
6. Hetou Village
7. Dongguaping Village
8. Heduimen Village

9. Shangzh ai Village
10. Dazhai Village
11. Nawang Village
12. Xinzhai Village

13. Dongkou Village
14. Nadie Village

1 XINA VILLAGE – Portal of Louna, Rebuild the Village Center

On the premise of protecting the texture of the original peak forest, farmland, and settlement, it aims to construct the functional service area at the entrance of Louna Tourist Attraction, and the demonstration zone of the scenic spot, which shall be built jointly by the villagers and citizens and with the characteristics of intelligence and internationalization. During the detailed design process, it shall be unfolded from the levels of "one point and one ring, two districts and two streets, as well as three core areas. "
Team: Dalian University of Technology

2 LAOWANGZHAI VILLAGE IN SHUANGSHAN – Natural Ecology, Livable Pastoral and Innovative Shuangshan

It tries to set out in the dual perspectives of internal and external resources of the village to explore and seek for an effective way that could suit for and stimulate the sustainable development of Shuangshan, proposes the development vision of natural ecology, livable pastoral and innovative Shuangshan, and designs the key projects to be initiated.
Team: Tsinghua University

3 DUSHAN VILLAGE – Agriculture plus Tourism

By following the "law of 5 percent", guided by the hydraulic engineering that supports the organic fruits and vegetables as well as the ecological breeding quality improvement, the design shall set the activation and utilization of the Stone Houses, the reconstruction and upgrading of the Water Houses, as well as the growth and spreading of the Green Houses as the catalyst. Through micro intervention and promoting work in all areas by drawing upon the experience gained on key points, it is intended to improve the living environment, and accelerate the combination between agriculture and tourism so as to show the great vitality.
Team: Kunming University of Science and Technology

4 HUJIAWAN VILLAGE – Louna Wonderland

The abandoned houses are mixed with the modern regional style, which are endowed with the functions of ancestral halls and architecture creation centers. The form and the spirit of integration of ancient and modern could be the catalyst for arousing the village spirit. The water diversion to the mountain slope would come back to the earth after the fulfillment of landscape architecture, fishery, water reservation, irrigation, and recycling use. To feed the chicken with the maggot from the toilet could be the "hot cake" due to its ecological high technology.
Team: Huazhong University of Science and Technology

5 ZHENGJIAYING VILLAGE – Flower Valley, A Secret Garden

It is supposed to improve the landscape and the living quality through controlling six environmental elements of walls, yards, farmlands, roads, waters, and bamboos. It is supposed to combine the public activity of double boxes with the children tree houses so as to offer equal opportunity for the village children to receive quality education through the internet.
Team: Institute of Shanghai Architectural Design and Research Co., Ltd.

6 HETOU VILLAGE – Upstream of Louna, Aroma of Hetou

The design is incorporated with the working strategy of "micro intervention, emphasis on tapping, slow in building houses, and prompt farmland reclaim," trying to reach the target of "tasting the aroma in Hetou Village in the upstream of Louna." It is supposed to co-construct a poetic and livable Hetou Village together with the villagers.
Team: Field Architecture Office

7 DONGGUAPING VILLAGE – Children-oriented Design

The design of Dongguaping is supposed to focus on the children and try to strike a balance between more and less, based on village structure. It shall activate the village with children-friendly design.
Team: Harbin Institute of Technology

8 HEDUIMEN VILLAGE – Village Fair: Rustic Shopping Haven

The design takes the village fair as the theme, constructs four fair modes of streets, yards, gardens, and waters in Heduimen village, and creates multiple spatial experiences for diverse groups of people. It also combines the product design of fishery, bridges, cultivation, and reading to drive rural revitalization.
Team: Tianjin University

9 SHANGZHAI VILLAGE – The Bouyei Living Room

According to the scheme, the image of the large house would be the arresting public space of the village. As the "living room" of the village, the continuous open space consists of the large house, space under the roof, and fore plaza. It is supposed to activate the space in a simple way and establish the hub for demonstrating the folk culture of the Bouyei people as well as for communications between communities.
Team: University of Chinese Academy of Sciences

10 DAZHAI VILLAGE – Village of Stone, Trip of Design

Dazhai Village preserves a large amount of intensive folk houses made of stones. The tourist route, called Trip of Design, passes through the wheat field at the entrance of the village, and mountains at the back of the village, connecting the folk houses with local characteristics together.
Team: Hunan University

11 NAWANG VILLAGE – Sketching Paradise

According to the natural geography as well as the cultural and historic features, and the positioning of the village of artists, the development theme of "painting paradise" tries to activate the traditional villages through autonomy of the villagers and industrial mode of continuous upgrading.
Team: Shenyang Jianzhu University

12 XINZHAI VILLAGE – Exploring Base of Primitive Hiking

The reconstruction of Xinzhai Village is supposed to focus on its abundant tourism resources and create two tourism routes, including the family trip and field hiking. It highlights the key space nodes, including the workshop for masters, Zhao's Restaurant, and landscape devices. In addition, it is supposed to provide the guidance and assistance for the villagers to carry out self-reconstruction in the future through the design guidelines.
Team: South China University of Technology

13 DONGKOU VILLAGE + DACHONG RESETTLEMENT AREA – Heritage of Folk Arts

It is intended to establish the mutual trust relationship with the villagers and stimulate the enthusiasm and involvement of the villagers to carry out the reconstruction of the infrastructure facilities, public service facilities, and living amenities. It is also supposed to gather the artisans through relevant competitions and build the tourist destination of Folk Arts + Folk Homes.
Team: Beijing Anzhe Architectural Design and Consulting Co., Ltd.

14 NADIE VILLAGE + DACHONG RESETTLEMENT AREA – Culture plus Ecology, Syncretic Country Life

Being positioned and guided by the concept of "culture plus ecology," it aims to construct the paradise of country life that integrates the village culture and the natural ecology. It will take the opportunity of village tourism, and integrate the entire process of the life and leisure experience, including dining, accommodation, sightseeing, traveling, and amusement, so as to improve the environment quality, inherit the folk culture, and promote economic development.
Team: Chongqing University

TOURIS

旅

M

The countryside is often considered as a place of imagination of nature, tradition, and history. Rural tourism is a typical manifestation of this imagination. Agritainment, homestays, experience farms, and hotels, are different forms of rural tourism services that indicate an increasingly divided and mature market. While the tourism economy greatly boosts local development, it also offers architects an opportunity to design with the considerations of nature, topography, state of mind, and tradition.

Tourism

Hua Li's **Xinzhai Coffee Manor** proposed a renovation as well as a new structure for the world's renowned arabica coffee in Lujiangba, Yunan Province. The use of local bricks creates different types of structural form and thus offers a spatial transition from the classical to the modern for the visitors. Naturalbuild and temp architects' tourist residences in the Zhejiang Province, **Lostvilla Boutique Hotel** and **Hotel of Septuor**, create a dialogue between the space and the natural environment. Both projects take advantage of existing features in the surroundings—centuries-old trees, distant mountains, natural terrain—and organize its space through a sequence of views. Also in Zhejiang Province, Zhang Lei designed a **Ruralation Shengaoli Library** for the tourist residence facility, which incorporates the renovation of an ancient hall from the Qing dynasty. The library opens to all villagers as a cultural and community center. Following a typical Tibetan layout, Zhang Li's **Jianamani Visitor Center** also serves tourists, pilgrims, and local villagers. While the building informs visitors of the history of Jianamani, it also provides basic community services such as post office, clinic, and public restroom.

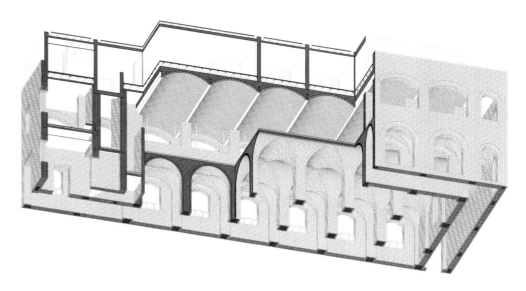

XINZHAI COFFEE MANOR SECTIONAL MODEL

Design team: Hua Li, Ma Kun
Fabricator: ZHONGKAI Model Making Firm
Material: Wood
Size: 2.9x0.9x1.7 meters

The installation uses hardwood to introduce the section on both sides of the building. We chose a 1:25 scale model to represent how architecture can revive the traditional coffee industry. Instead of designing an abstract art installation, the architectural manifestation is a way to indicate how architecture can respond to context.

Brick structure of Xinzhai Coffee Manor

XINZHAI COFFEE MANOR

Hua Li | Trace Architecture Office

Location: Bawan Village, Baoshan, Yunnan
Architect: Trace Architecture Office (TAO)
Principal architect: Hua Li
Design team: Hua Li, Bai Ting, Lai Erxun, Hu Mohuai, Zhang Wenzhao, Yue Yang, Zhang Hao, Liu Zhouxing
Structure: Concrete and masonry structure
Area: 3140 square meters (new construction: 2000 square meters; renovation: 1140 square meters)
Design period: 2014–2015
Construction period: Commenced in 2015

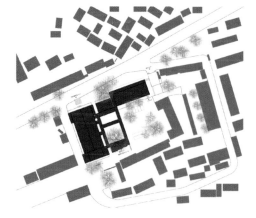

Site plan

The project is located in Lujiangba, Baoshan, Yunnan Province, which is recognized worldwide as producing the best arabica coffee. Commissioned by the owner of a local coffee brand, TAO proposed a renovation and new construction on the wooded high ground, hoping to engage visitors with a pleasant architectural experience that matches the high quality of arabica coffee and the beautiful surrounding environment.

Hidden by existing trees, the old and new buildings together with the cloister form a variety of functional spaces. Local bricks and concrete were used as the main construction materials to create different types of structural forms, and thus a rich set of harmonious interiors and exterior spaces for different programs.

The storage warehouse is located at the bottom floor of the main building. Constructed with a series of cross vaults, the space meets the storage requirements of maintaining constant temperature and humidity for coffee beans, while at the same time creating an engaging atmosphere. Located on the first floor, the manufacturing area required space for roasting and packaging coffee beans, as well as conducting visitor tours. The design incorporated large-span steel girders with brick archways to form a set of continuous spaces. Guest rooms, located on the top floor, provide open views of the valley with plain, open concrete frames. From bottom to top, there is a transition from the classical to the modern, responding to the diverse needs of storage, manufacturing, and scenery viewing.

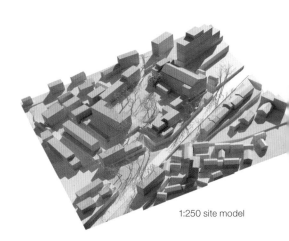

1:250 site model

Warehouse with classical arches

1:100 model of first floor

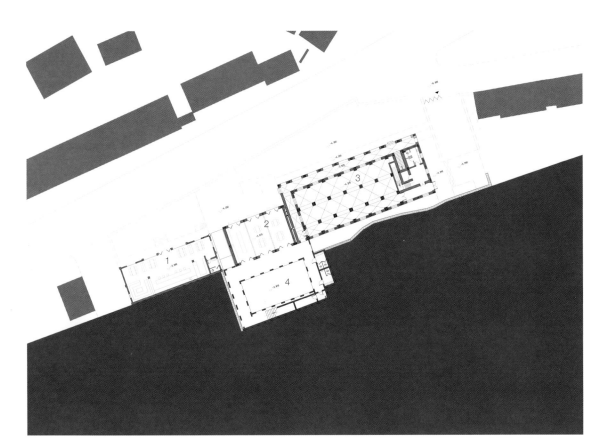

Basement floor plan

1. VIP cupping
2. Café
3. Coffee warehouse
4. Sunken courtyard

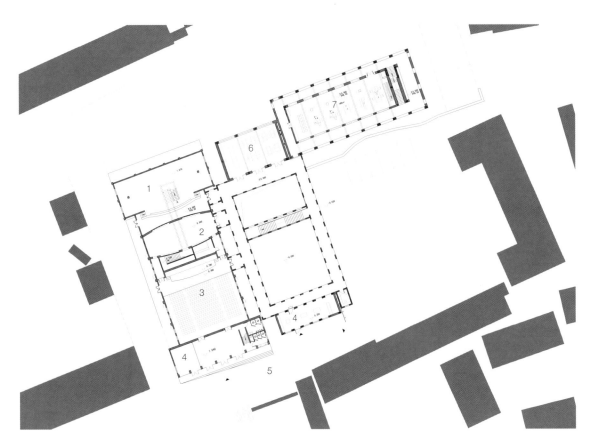

First-floor plan

1. Exhibition room
2. Foyer
3. Conference room
4. Shop
5. Theatre entrance
6. Café
7. Coffee processing zone

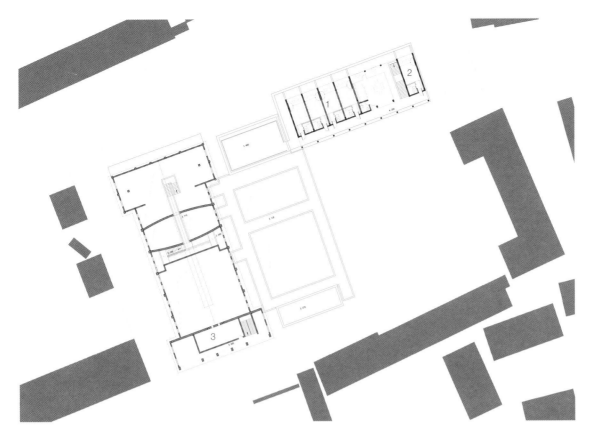

Second-floor plan

1. Guest room
2. VIP lounge
3. Storage

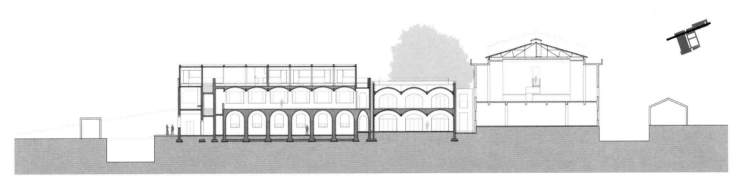

Section A

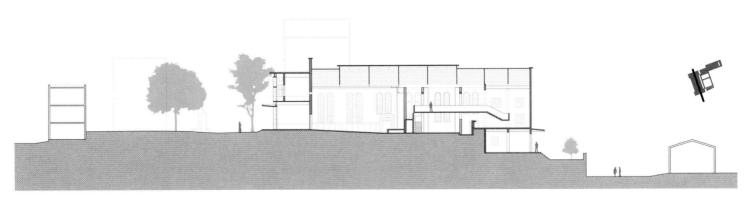

Section B

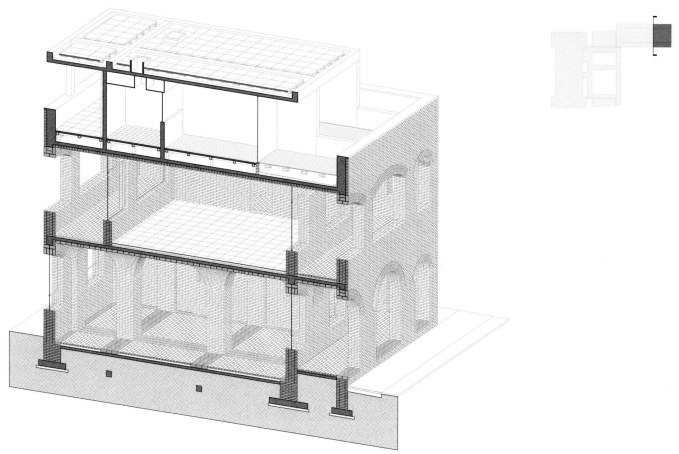

Sectional axonometric drawing of guesthouse and warehouse

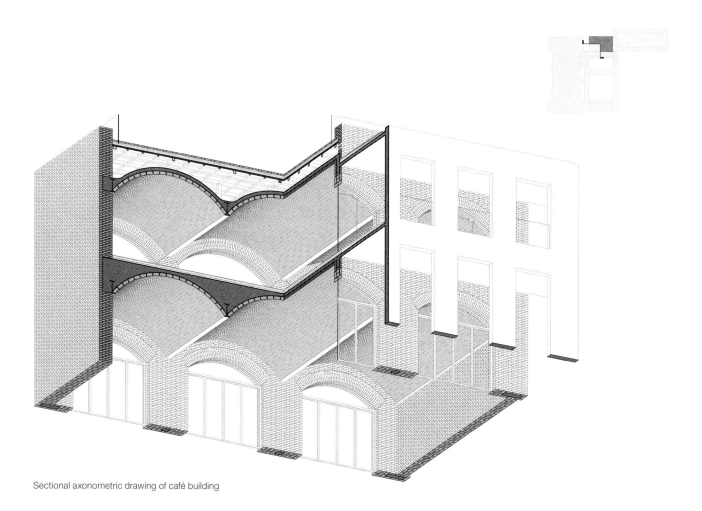

Sectional axonometric drawing of café building

Wall

1. Elevated plate (@ 7.410 m)
2. Structure soffit (@ 6.950 m)
3. Ceiling (@ 6.450 m)
4. Guest room (@ 4.250 m)
5. Arch crown with built-in exhaust pipe (@ 3.500 m)
6. Steel beam soffit (@ 2.875 m)
7. Windowsill (@ 0.875 m)
8. Arch springing (@ -1.875 m)
9. Arch crown (@ -0.375 m)
10. Warehouse (@ -4.375 m)

$\dfrac{1}{\dfrac{2}{3}}$

1. 1:100 model second floor
2. 1:100 model first floor
3. 1:100 model basement

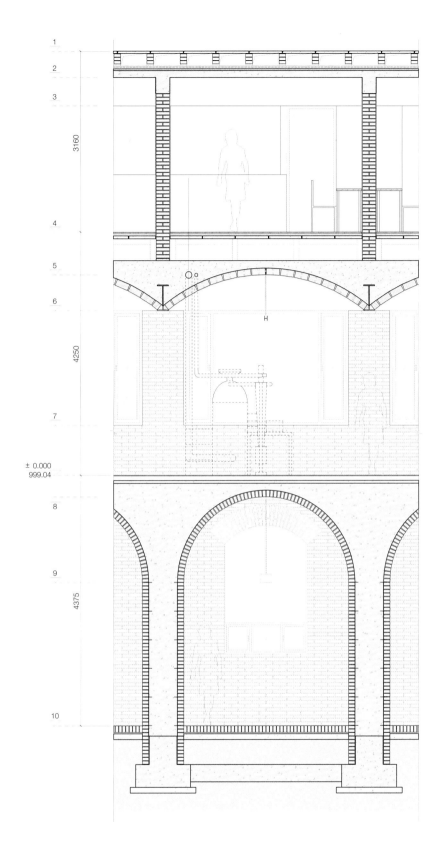

RURALATION SHENAOLI LIBRARY

Zhang Lei | AZL Architects

Location: Tonglu, Zhejiang Province, China
Architect: Zhang Lei, AZL Architects
Project team: Zhang Lei, Ma Haiyi, Wu Guanzhong,
Ren Zhuqing, Du Yue, Feng Qi
Area: 1000 square meters
Project period: December 2014–October 2015
Photography: Yao Li, AZL Architects

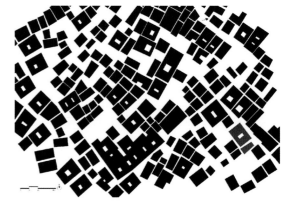

Site plan

Ruralation Shenaoli Library is located in the ancient village of Shenao, Jiangan, Tonglu, Hangzhou, and was the first completed work by Eshan practice. The village is developed together with the Shentu clan and has a storied history of more than 1900 years. This ancient village is adjacent to Tonglu, a country town 30-minutes' drive from Hangzhou. The village's unique underground spring and drains have been well-conserved, as have more than 40 historic buildings constructed during the Ming and Qing dynasties.

Jingsong Hall, an ancient house constructed during the late Qing dynasty, forms the main body of this project. In addition, the restoration of surrounding vernacular dwellings has also been taken into consideration. The structures' historic texture is expressed in their façades, and the traditional architectural layout and exquisite timber carving have been preserved.

In this way, a comfortable, contemporary interior space has been realized. From the standpoint of design and construction, the knowledge and building techniques of local craftsmen have been strongly respected—the architect learned construction skills from local craftsmen. Also, local craftsmen conducted a "construction performance" using different props under the instruction of the architect.

Ruralation Shenaoli contains a community library open to all villagers, a "culture and folk traditions" exhibition space, and homestays. Together, these rich functions and spaces make the bookstore an ideal space for entertaining tourists, providing recreation options, and facilitating communication among villagers. It is a salon for the soul in which one can relive the memories of one's hometown and feel a sense of belonging to the community.

Entrance square

Guest room courtyard and entrance hall

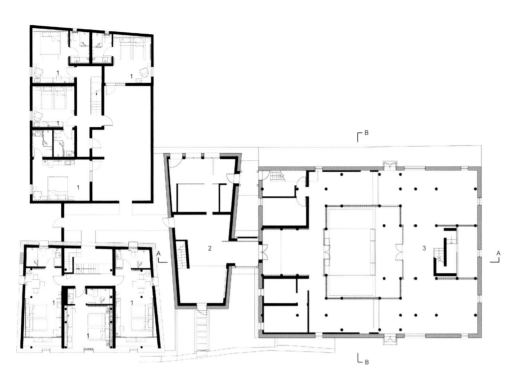

First-floor plan

1. Guest room
2. Lobby
3. Library cafeteria

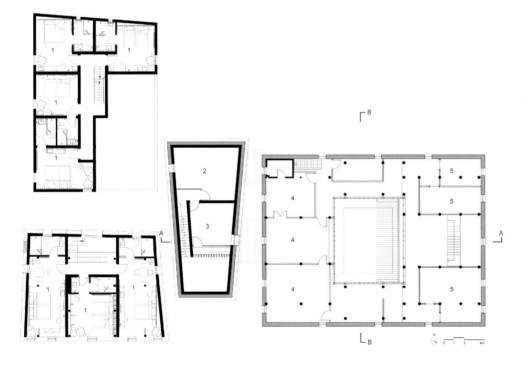

Second-floor plan

1. Guest room
2. Office
3. Equipment room
4. Conference
5. Loge

Street façade

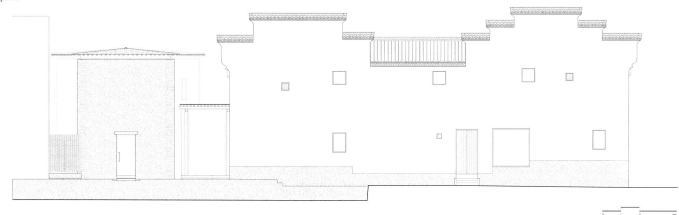

Elevation

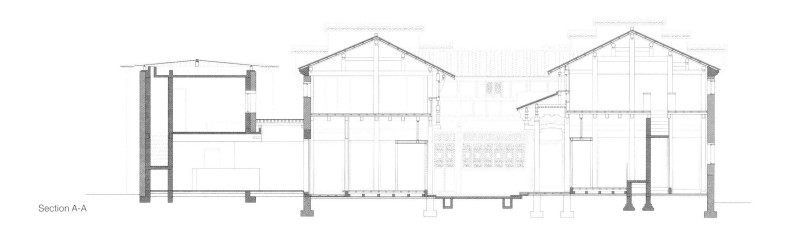

Section A-A

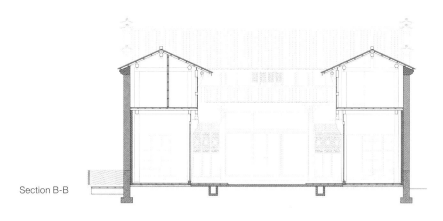

Section B-B

Jingsongtang restoration

LOSTVILLA BOUTIQUE HOTEL IN YUCUN

Shui Yanfei + Ma Yuanrong + Su Yichi | Naturalbuild

Location: No. 85, West Huangfu Street, Moganshan Town, Deqing County, Huzhou City, Zhejiang Province
Architect: Shui Yanfei, Su Yichi, Ma Yuanrong
Principal architects: Naturalbuild
Project architects: Deng Dan, Xu Hanhua
Project team: Li Gege, Sun Jing, Chai Xini, Zhou Xiaoyan, Wang Keyi, Chen Hao, Luo Linlin, Chen Zhuoran, Zhu Lijin, Lv Yuan, Jeffery Wong, Zhu Ying
Structural consultant: Zhang Zhun
Engineering consultant: Chen Zhe, Lu Pengfei, Chen Qiang
Structure: Mixed masonry structure, wood and steel truss
Area: 1735 square meters (site); 1491 square meters (building)
Design period: March 2015–June 2017
Construction period: October 2015–June 2017
Photography: Chen Hao

Site plan

Located at the southwest corner of a previously state-owned silkworm farm in Yucun, Moganshan, Zhejiang Province, the project is connected to the peak of Mogan Mountain by a mountain trail. The site can be accessed from the northwest corner, and the terrain slopes gradually down from north to south. There are cottages with jagged outline standing adjacent to the north, whereas the southern end opens to a panoramic view of a meandering stream.

The design is therefore constrained and motivated by both the dynamic present and the unpredictable future. The strategy of internalizing scenery not only served as a defensive gesture against the unfavorable surrounding conditions, but also turned the saturated inner space into part of the landscape. At the same time, the design provides a series of public programs for locals, such as a café (with its own entrance separate from the hotel), a small exhibition area, and a restaurant on the third floor. The arrangement of programs creates a unique circulation between public spaces and hotel areas and offers a variety of experiences for strolling around.

Most of the guest rooms are in the southern part of the main building to obtain sufficient sunlight and provide panoramic scenic views of the garden. At the west end, a loggia and a swimming pool frame the main entrance and create a perimeter that buffers the site from the main road. The loggia, together with the main building, forms an open backyard area that serves only hotel guests.

Taking advantage of the site's centuries-old camphor and the Platanus tree, as well as the distant mountains, the design frames scenes to create a sequence of dynamic views from the building. The framing scenery interacts differently with the layout of each individual room and diversifies the relationships between each room's plan and window. It also interacts differently with the program-matic layout and diversifies the relationship between the interior plan and window, allow-ing strategic thinking of specificity to surpass the monopoly of a concept. In the end, the design offers a more natural posture.

The design aims to achieve a type of optical precision; not the precision of construction details, but rather that which creates a dialogue between details and the background scenery. On the one hand, the details of the design process aim to respond to typical problems that one encounters when building in rural China. These include poor construction quality,

Street view from northwest side

lack of infrastructure, and limited product supply. These respective issues were resolved through a close collaborative process that spanned design, construction, and development, and involved (the designers), prefabrication suppliers, and local craftsmen. A series of steel and wood window and door systems, interior plywood doors, extra-large automatic windows, and customized light fixtures and furniture are products of this collaborative effort. On the other hand, other details of the design are reactions to inevitable construction errors and sudden changes of local constraints. These accidents induced a series of impromptu, on-site designs.

View west and the Platnaus tree

Third-floor plan

Second-floor plan

First-floor plan

1. Café
2. Public courtyard
3. Lobby
4. Guest room
5. Kitchen
6. Hotel courtyard
7. Loggia
8. Pool
9. Meeting room
10. Storage
11. Restaurant
12. Servery

0   5   15 MTS

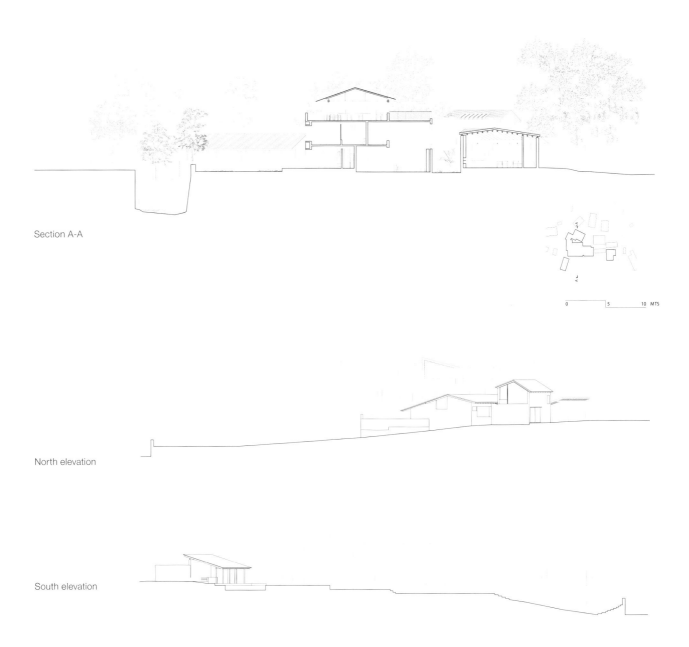

Section A-A

0   5   10 MTS

North elevation

South elevation

Café and main building

Loggia on the southwest side and main building

JIANAMANI VISITOR CENTER

Zhang Li | Atelier TeamMinus

Location: Yushu Tibetan Autonomous Prefecture, Qinghai Province
Architect: Zhang Li
Structure: Sheer wall
Area: 3591 square meters (site); 1147 square meters (building)
Design period: September 2010–October 2011
Construction period: October 2011–November 2012

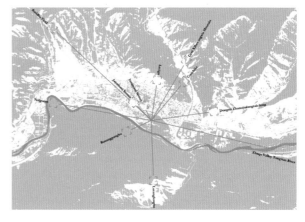

Site plan

Yushu is a highly regarded by Tibetans as religious center. Its significance stems mainly from Jianamani, the world's largest Tibetan Buddhist cairn. With a history of more than three centuries, Jianamani currently contains upwards of 250 million pieces of Mani stones, and is growing daily as pilgrims add new pieces.

In Yushu, more the 40 percent of the population make a living carving Mani stones. To the Yushu community, nothing compares to Jianamani. After the 2010 earthquake, Yushu residents set off immediately to repair Jianamani, long before their own houses.

Jianamani Visitor Center serves both visitors and the local community. To visitors and pilgrims, it provides information about Jianamani and its history, complemented by views of the site itself. For local residents, it provides a post office, clinic, restroom, and small research archive.

Jianamani Visitor Center is a square building with a courtyard in the center and 11 observation decks surrounding it. The central square volume features the typical Tibetan layout. Of the 11 observation decks, two point to Jianamani, while the remaining nine face historic and religious sites related to Jianamani, including: Leciga, Genixi Bawang Xiou, Cuochike, Dongna Zhunatalang Taiqinleng, Zhaqu River Valley, Lazanglongba, Rusongongbu, Naigu River Beach, and Kuanyin Rebirth Site.

Jianamani Visitor Center was built primarily using local construction techniques. Stone-masonry was done by local masons, using the same kind of rock from which Mani stones are carved. The railings around the roof terrace and the observation decks were made from wood, including elements recycled from earthquake debris.

Overall massing

View from the corridor

Monks in front of the visiting center

First-floor plan

1. Electric power distribution
2. Gift shop
3. Bank
4. Public telephone
5. Post
6. Clinic
7. Public restroom
8. Courtyard

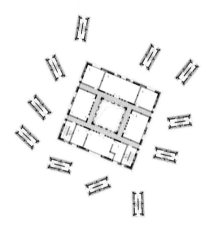

Second-floor plan

1. Exhibition
2. Research archive
3. Office
4. Police substation

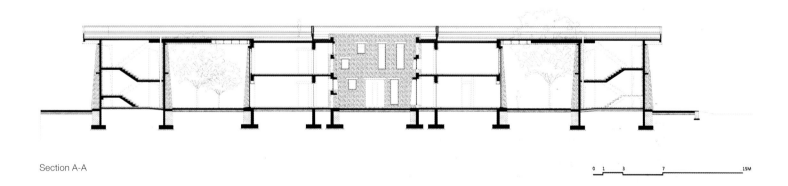

Section A-A

Detail

1. Treated external flooring boards, 50x30 mm treated timber batten spacing at 400 mm crs, 100x100 mm treated timber, 80 mm C20 steel and concrete with <PB steel spacing at 200 mm crs, OAmm waterproof membrane, waterproof membrane wrap, min 20 mm, max 70 mm concrete floor level

2. Structural steel concrete floor, L40 steel angle plate to structural steel, I40 steel angle plate, 40x40 mm treated timber batten, 900x150x15 mm treated timber boards to steel angle plate

3. 50x50 mm fixed on the side angle wall, L30 planks attached to the angle

4. Transverse wire-rope aluminum windows and doors of the same material package flooring

5. Mortar to smooth finish

6. 200 mm 1:2.5 water cement to smooth finish, 1 mm rubber water cement, 150 mm C15 steel concrete flooring, smooth finish to internal concrete ceiling

7. 20 mm 1:2.5 water cement to smooth finish, 1 mm rubber water cement, 150 mm C15 steel concrete flooring

8. 20 mm 1:2.5 water cement to smooth finish

9. 300x300x50 mm granite floor with 1:1 cement to seal

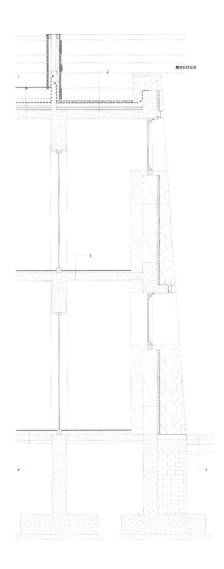

Detail

1. 900x145x20 mm treated timber flooring boards, 50x30 mm treated timber batten spacing at 400 mm crs, 100x100x20 mm treated timber, 80 mm C20 steel and concrete with <P8 steel spacing at 200 mm crs, 0.4 mm waterproof membrane wrap, 20mm 1:2.5 water cement level, min 40 mm, max 200 mm concrete floor level, 800 mm polystyrene insulation board, 20 mm 1:2.5 water cement level, structural steel and concrete floor

2. 80 mm pebble stone to level, one layer waterproof membrane, 3 mm waterproof membrane wrap, min 20 mm, max 70 mm concrete floor level, 80 mm polystyrene insulation board, 20 mm 1:2.5 water cement level, structural and steel concrete floor

3. 12mm interior tongue-and-groove timber flooring board sealed to finish, 35 mm floor rubber base, 35 mm 1:2.5 water cement pressed firm to level, 1 mm rubber water cement, 150 mm C15 steel concrete floor

4. 12 mm interior tongue-and-groove timber flooring board sealed to finish, 3 to 5 mm floor rubber base, 85 mm C20 concrete gravel pressed firm to level, 150 mm C15 concrete pressed firm to level, land fill pressed firm to level at ratio 0.90

5. 300x300x50 mm granite floor with 1:1 cement to steel

HOTEL OF SEPTUOR

Wang Fangji + Dong Xiao +Xiao Xiao | temp architects

Location: Deqing, Zhejiang, China
Principal architects: Wang Fangji, Dong Xiao, Xiao Xiao
Project team: Zhang Ting, Chen Changshan, Qian Chen, Lin Jing, Liu Yunong, Wu Enting
Area: 645 square meters (built area)
Design and construction period: 2015–2017
Photography: temp architects, Zhong Hai

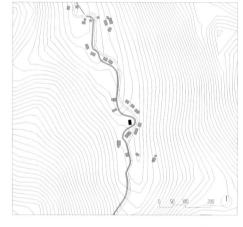

Site plan

Hotel of Septuor is a seven-room boutique hotel located in a valley among the hills of Deqing. Adjacent to the Yangtze River Delta, this region is a leisure destination characteristic of the classic bamboo-forest landscape. The valley runs south to north with a stream parallel to the road and houses built alongside.

The hotel is located where the stream loops out in a semicircular curve to form a peninsula. The site was carefully selected. The hotel was renovated from a local dwelling, a typical two-story timber structures with double-pitched roofs and loam walls. To transform a compact village house into a spacious hotel, the original structural skeleton was revised and the width of each room reorganized. The wooden pillars standing independently from the partition walls suggest the previous structure. A new concrete structure was added parallel to the old one to accommodate bathrooms and other facilities.

To create an intimate relationship between the living space and the natural environment, the original linear corridor system was reshaped into various paths and staircases leading to each of the seven rooms. Public spaces, such as the entrance lobby, café, meeting rooms, and dining spaces, are integrated into the structure, and the roof of these new volumes is used as private terrace gardens for guest rooms on the second floor. To make the most of the backyard, a new rounded guest room was built. A cone-shaped skylight and an ear-shaped partition with a pale golden color create a fluid and mysterious atmosphere.

The site's natural terrain and paths were preserved and extended into the inner space. The different spaces are organized in a continuous sequence with circular pathways on the ground floor. The overall character of the building is open and inviting, while the separate rooms and gardens are quiet and intimate.

Overall aerial view

Guest room 4

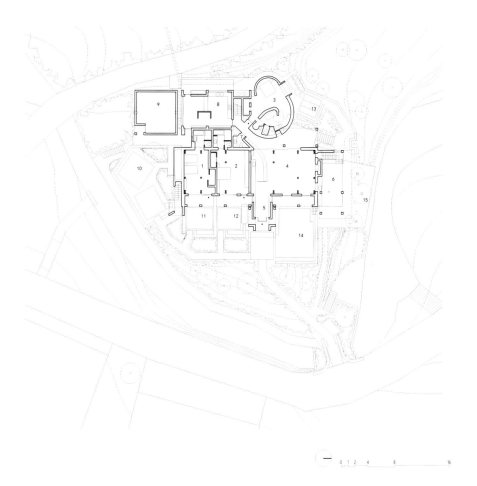

First-floor plan

1. Guest room 1
2. Guest room 2
3. Guest room 3
4. Entrance lobby
5. Hallway
6. Café
7. Public restroom
8. Kitchen
9. Landlord's house
10. Southern public terrace
11. Garden for guest room 1
12. Garden for guest room 2
13. Garden for guest room 3
14. Eastern public terrace
15. Public terrace for café

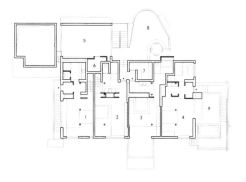

Second-floor plan

1. Guest room 4
2. Guest room 5
3. Guest room 6
4. Guest room 7
5. Meeting and dining space
6. Storage room
7. Linen room
8. Public terrace
9. Garden for guest room 7

Third-floor plan

1. Bathroom for guest room 4
2. Bathroom for guest room 5
3. Garden for guest room 4
4. Garden for guest room 5

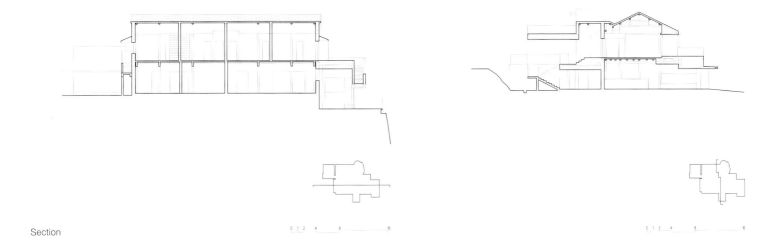

Section

Detail

1. Anticorrosive wooden board (seat)
2. Anticorrosive wooden board (floor)
3. Anticorrosive wooden board (wall)
4. Gray clay roof tile
5. Stainless steel gutter
6. Bamboo light slot
7. Sewage pipe
8. Terrazzo
9. Sarking
10. Existing rafter
11. Existing pillar
12. Mirror
13. Waterproofing latex paint
14. PVC pipe with gold-colored paint
15. Existing beam
16. New pillar
17. LED strip
18. Existing wooden floor
19. Reinforced-concrete floor
20. Oak wooden board
21. Rough stone wall
22. Vent pipe
23. Reinforced concrete
24. Tempered glass
25. Diatom mud in white color
26. Diatom mud in golden color
27. Sliding door
28. Ventilator
29. Tempered glass
30. Insulated corrugated-steel plate
31. New rafter

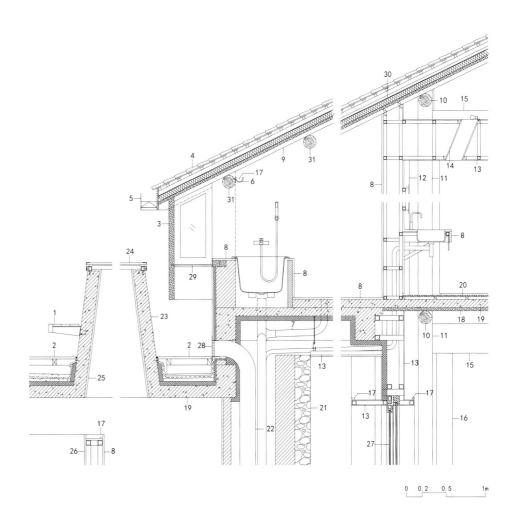

BEYOND MOGAN MOUTAIN

Jin Jiangbo | Shanghai Academy of Fine Arts

Director: Jin Jiangbo
Producer: Shen Yaoteng
Executive director and cinematographer: Yan Siwen, Zhao Ning

Aerial view of tea plantation area of Mogan Mountain

With the transformation and development of rural areas, Mogan Mountain, as a tourist destination, has become famous for its beautiful environment, rich culture, and convenient transportation. The area is usually considered a "back garden" for Shanghai. Since the period of the Republic of China, it has been the holiday destination for nobles and celebrities. Nowadays, it is a resort to enjoy a slow-paced life for those who live in cities and prefers a natural environment. In the past decade, many artists, architects, and creative workers have come to Mogan Mountain and transformed the villagers' old houses into modern living spaces. Mogan Mountain's ecological environment, local characteristics, and the comprehensive renovation of residential areas are all integrated interpretations of the area as an effective supplement to urban cultural life. Through artistic approaches in rural field work, Shanghai Academy of Fine Arts has carried out its research program in Mogan Mountain. With the advantages of artistic disciplines and intellectual talents, the university will explore a sustainable development path for the countryside based on local public life and tradition.

Aerial view of Mogan Mountain

1. Locals picking tea leaves
2. Learning local craft
3. Bamboo weaving craft

COMMU

NITY 社

In today's countryside, traditional ethic orders and modernization have been intertwining, giving rise to new demands. Architecture empowers public space with orders and flexibility and provides a stable foundation for rural lives, where interrelational, ecological, and social factors are coherent. Participators and users also creatively adapt the functions of public buildings to adjust them for different needs. Architecture eventually becomes a cooperating and coexisting space for community development, activities, and governance.

Community

Rural Urban Framework's **Andong Hospital** is a rural healthcare facility and a community center. A continuous ramp that connects programmatic spaces also acts as a new public space. While recycled brick is used in its façade, the design also recycles tradition for today. A similar strategy is employed in the office's installation **An Old-new House**, which reuses materials from an abandoned wooden house in rural Yunan Province and is reassembled into a viewing tower for celebration events. Atelier Deshaus creates a village within the village of Xinchang in **Xinchang Central Kindergarten**, sponsored by One Foundation. Nine isolated cottages form an inner courtyard, which is both a playground for children and a space of connections. The significance of the courtyard as a community space is also a focus in Zhao Yang's **Chaimiduo Farm Restaurant and Bazaar**.

An operable bamboo-façade panel creates greater interaction between the interior and the courtyard. **Lukou Grameen Village Bank** is a community center for rural financial aid. With the NewBud building system, developed by architect Zhu Jingxiang and his team, the design and construction processes took only eight weeks and most of the assembly work was done by locals. While the above projects act as social infrastructure for the making of a community, physical infrastructure is also crucial to the countryside. Both Fu Yingbin's **Tongzi Pedestrian Bridge** and Xu Tiantian's **Shimen Bridge** creates connections that are otherwise severed by natural landscape. In addition to that, by taking advantage of local construction techniques and typologies, they are also social spaces for locals.

1. Village aerial view
2. Old house
3. Old house dismantled
4. Old-new House
5. Construction

AN OLD-NEW HOUSE: RECYCLING THE RURAL

Architect: Rural Urban Framework

Design team: John Lin, Joshua Bolchover, Liu Chang, Timothy Robert, Chiara Oggioni.

Size: 6x6x6 meters

Materials: Recycled timber from abandoned wooden house in Zhaotong, Yunnan.

Throughout China, the urbanization process in developing areas has led to vast amounts of construction of generic building types using standardized materials. Alongside this construction process is the simultaneous demolition of old fabric, deemed unsuitable by government bureaus and villagers in China's era of modernization. Rather than reverting to a nostalgia for lost craftsmanship or for a Chinese architectural identity, our approach to the issue of rural urbanization is demonstrating the ability of design to repurpose tradition for the use of a modern community.

At the Venice Biennale, we propose a 1:1 construction that recycles the material from an abandoned wooden house in rural Yunnan province into a viewing tower during the Chinese New Year. After hosting the New Year celebration, the structure will be shipped to Venice and installed as a symposium venue. The reconstruction of a private house into a public venue, a traditional structure into a modern context, will echo our belief in the vitality of the current rural situation and the necessity of the architect's participation in the rural to urban transformation of China.

Celebration during the Chinese New Year

ANGDONG HOSPITAL

John Lin + Joshua Bolchover | Rural Urban Framework

Location: Baojing County, Hunan Province, China
Architects: Joshua Bolchover and John Lin, Rural Urban Framework
Project manager: Maggie K. Y. Ma
Project team: Mark Kingsley, Jeffery Huang, Crystal Kwan, Huang Zhiyun, Tiffany Leung, Johnny Cullinan, Tanya Tsui, Joyce Ip
Area: 1450 square meters
Commission date: May 2011
Commissioning donor: Institute of Integrated Rural Development
Additional donor: Luke Him Sau Charitable Trust

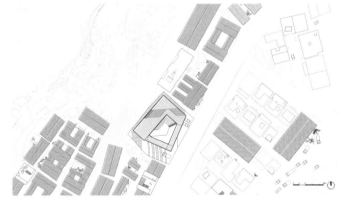

Site plan

The Angdong Hospital project proposes that the rural healthcare building is a center of community life in an urbanizing town center. The design strategy utilizes recycled bricks from a nearby factory to create a continuous ramp access that functions as a new public space. Today, elderly and children use the spaces of the hospital for exercise and play. The Angdong Hospital project challenges the generic architecture of the institution through programmatic and material innovation.

Commissioned by Hong Kong charity Institute for Integrated Rural Development and working closely with the local health bureau, our task was to develop a model rural healthcare building capable of supporting the many progressive reforms of rural hospital management and caregiving. This includes providing necessities absent in current establishments, some as simple as waiting rooms, and offering both traditional Chinese and Western medicine. Additionally, seeing that most institutions in China are gated and privatized, we were interested in introducing the hospital as a public building in the heart of the village.

The form of the hospital was generated in response to the need to have an accessible ramp to all floors. The phasing strategy proposed the existing hospital be kept in use until the new building had been built, and then demolished and a ramp inserted as the last component to connect all the floors. This ramp wraps an inner courtyard forming a public space leading to the roof. The ramp and rooftop are publicly accessible, serving as a common meeting space and play space for children. On the ground level, the courtyard extends into the natural slope, creating additional steps for seating as an outdoor waiting area.

Angdong Hospital is innovated in creating variation and specificity with a generic material. We took on the typical concrete-screen block ubiquitous across China that comprises a square block with a circular void in the middle. We developed a flexible casting mold that could vary the orientation and distance of extrusion or intrusion of this aperture. Through experimentation, we selected three types for their filtration effect and viewing direction. Having developed and cast prototypes in Hong Kong, these were taken to the fabricator—a local villager in Angdong—as the positives, from which fiberglass molds were fabricated for massproduction. The exterior envelope was constructed from discarded gray bricks made available through the recent demolition of a brick factory. These were arranged in fins placed at a 45-degree angle so that from some viewpoints the buildings appear as a solid mass and from others the interior is revealed.

Aerial view of Angdong Hospital

In contrast, the deployment of the screen blocks on the inner courtyard façade created a softer, variegated surface filtering light and offering different vistas as one traverses the ramp.

Angdong Hospital exemplifies our work to challenge generic forms and material applications. Through the tactics of programmatic organization, reuse of materials, and invention, we aim to create unique public buildings in rural China.

Angdong Hospital roofscape

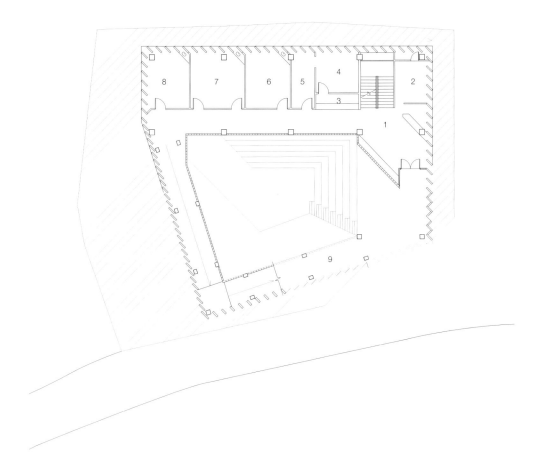

First-floor plan

1. Waiting area
2. Reception
3. Prescription
4. Western pharmacy and dressings room
5. Chinese pharmacy
6. Chinese medicine clinic
7. General clinic and examination room
8. Injections room
9. Ramp corridor

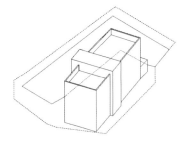

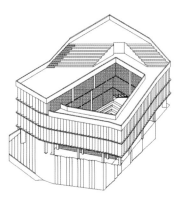

Phasing strategy

1. The old hospital building had no lift. Patients had to be carried up the stairs on their relatives' backs.

2. The new hospital was built around the old building. The old building continued to function during construction.

3. The old building was demelished and replaced by a public courtyard and ramp, allowing patients in wheelchairs to access the upper floors.

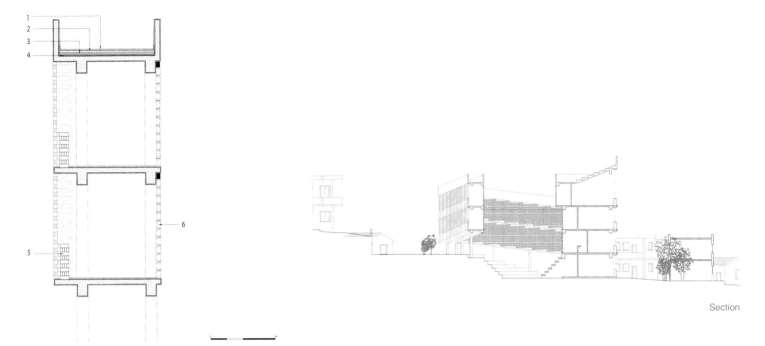

Detailed ramp section

1. Concrete screed
2. Waterproofing layer
3. Insulation board
4. 20 mm rock asphalt laid in three coats
5. Recycled brick wall
6. Custom-made concrete block

Section

Façade mock-up

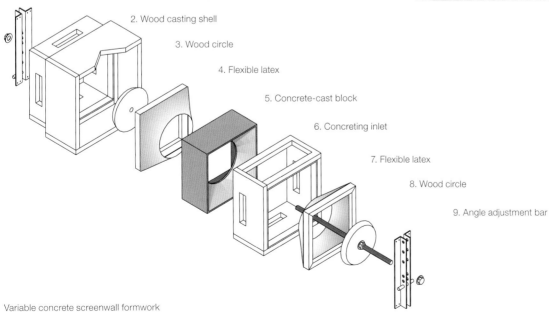

1. Angle adjustment bar

2. Wood casting shell

3. Wood circle

4. Flexible latex

5. Concrete-cast block

6. Concreting inlet

7. Flexible latex

8. Wood circle

9. Angle adjustment bar

Variable concrete screenwall formwork

Andong Hospital courtyard

Courtyard panorama

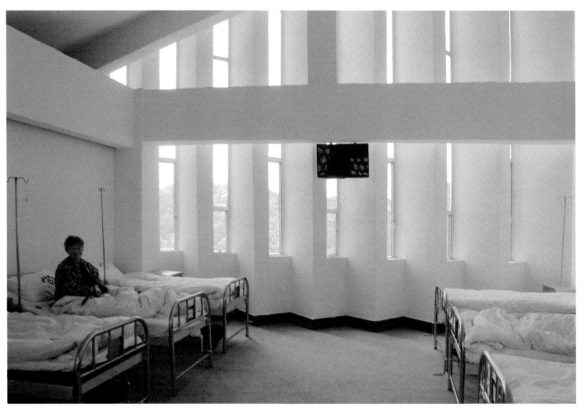

Patient room

Access ramp

XINCHANG VILLAGE CENTRAL KINDERGARTEN

SPONSORED BY ONE FOUNDATION

Chen Yifeng + Liu Yichun | Atelier Deshaus

Location: Xinchang Village, Tianquan County, Sichuan Province
Architect: Atelier Deshaus
Design team: Chen Yifeng, Liu Yichun, Gao Lin, Gao De
Construction: Beijing Tongchengfanghua Architecture & Engineering
Consulting Co., Ltd.
Area: 1500 square meters
Design period: 2014–2015
Project completion: 2017
Photography: Su Shengliang

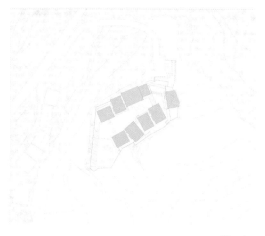

Site plan

Xinchang Village Kindergarten is one of more than 10 kindergartens that One Foundation has donated to the disaster area of the 2013 Lushan earthquake. Surrounded by mountains, the site is a relatively small platform northwest of the village. It faces a mountain gap to the west, giving visitors a sense of distance. The surrounding settlements, in addition to providing shelter for their inhabitants, subtly confront nature's domination. To maintain this peaceful, tranquil, and rustic atmosphere, new building must embrace the homey, local style.

The entire kindergarten was conceived as a "village." The total volume of 1500 square meters was divided into nine isolated "cottages" corresponding to different programs. These are located on the north, south, and east sides of the site, enclosing a U-shaped courtyard

facing west. The courtyard paving and building façades utilize locally produced sintered shale bricks, endowing the place with a strong sense of artificiality. Hence, on the one hand, the design stands apart from nature, while on the other hand, it forms an inseparable ensemble with the sky, the platform, the nearby villages, and the distant mountain gap.

Here, the sense of dimensions is spatial and temporal. The expression of nature is controlled and deeply related to the development and transformations of the site. The inner courtyard is the center of the kindergarten, as well as the kernel of its sense of directions and identity. Day by day, as children play in the courtyard, it will become the origin of affinity with the kindergarten and memories. The courtyard is the source of feelings of affiliation.

The design also took serious consideration of children's mental and physical characteristics, making efforts to realize the diversity and capability of playfulness in spatial typologies. Because Ya'an experiences heavy rainfall, the separate units of the kindergarten and the main entrance are connected by a circular veranda. This veranda adapts to the level differences of the site, cooperating with the ramp and stairs to create an intimate layer between the courtyard and the architecture, and providing additional possibilities for children's daily activities.

Limited by a relatively tight budget, the design must consider local construction and crafting abilities. The authenticity and autonomy of nearby villages provided us with a good reference. Since mean annual precipitation in the region can reach 2000 millimeters, a waterproof

Night view of the inner plaza

structure is essential. As the unit buildings of the kindergarten are not large, it was believed single-pitched roofs would drain efficiently and be convenient to construct. In terms of façade treatment, we used a sintered shale brick wall on top of a wall-filled frame to resist water. Shale brick, a common rustic material, is much better at repelling water than ordinary wall paints.

Overall view

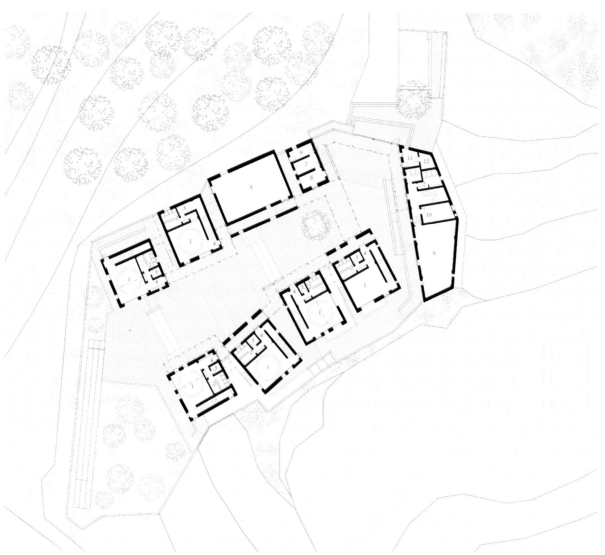

First-floor plan

1. Playroom
2. Bathroom
3. Storage room
4. Foyer
5. Major activity room
6. Observation ward
7. Health service
8. Examination room
9. Kitchen
10. Meeting room
11. Safety guard
12. Equipment

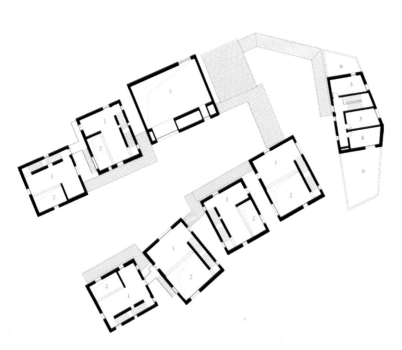

Second-floor plan

1. Bedroom
2. Void
3. Office
4. Principal office
5. Void
6. Terrace

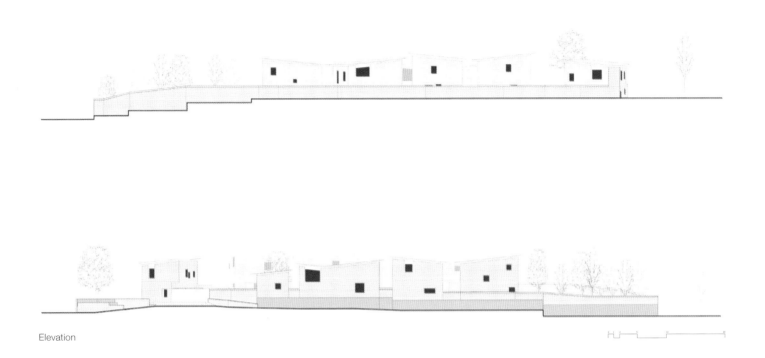

Elevation

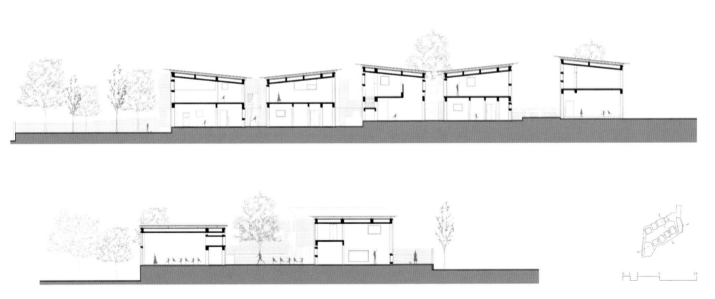

Section

East end of inner plaza

Axonometric diagram

Side corridor

LUKOU GRAMEEN VILLAGE BANK

Zhu Jingxiang | The Chinese University of Hong Kong

Location: Xinyi, Jiangsu Province, China
Project architects: Zhu Jingxiang, Xia Heng, Han Guori
Construction managers: Xia Heng, Han Guori, Zhao Yan
Supports: Peng Qiang
Structure: LGS skeleton strengthened by rigid board (NewBud system)
Manufacturer: Factories in Jiangsu Province
Earthquake resistance: VIII (Mercalli intensity scale)
Area: 200 square meters
Construction period: 18 days (superstructure), 10 days (base and landscape)
Project year: 2014

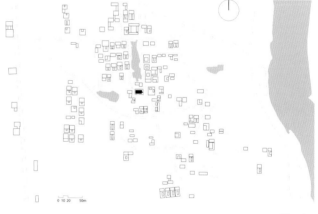

Site plan

In May 2014, Professor Muhammad Yunus, a Bangladeshi banker and economist who was awarded the Nobel Peace Prize, launched "Grameen China" to provide a guide for Chinese companies on how to follow the operation mode for social enterprise advocated by him. With Yunus's authorization, Mr. Gao Zhan, the chief executive officer of Yunus China Center, used his own funds to launch a new attempt in his hometown—Lukou Village, Xuzhou, Jiangsu Province. In November 2014, the research team from the School of Architecture of CUHK was invited to build Yunus China Center Grameen Village Bank in Lukou.

This 220-square-meter landmark takes the form of a typical northern Jiangsu rural home. Functioning as a community center for rural financial aid, the building also provides flexible spaces for a variety of activities, such as gathering, praying, performing, teaching, and training. South of the building is a square providing a communal space. Its public attributes and multifunctional character define it as a sustainable engine for rural development.

The NewBud building system applied in the construction consists of a light-gauge steel skeleton and a composite envelope. It provides a comprehensive and integrated solution to the multifaceted problem of inadequate heating, lighting, ventilation, and energy found in local buildings, and is particularly suitable for remote rural areas and regions with cold winters and hot summers. The elaborate design of the building's openings provides optimized ventilation.

Through elaborate planning and a distributed manufacturing program, the design and construction processes took only eight weeks. All building elements were produced within Jiangsu Province, and most of the assembly work was done by locals. Auxiliary utilities and ground paving was achieved using only local materials and techniques.

In addition to introducing new building techniques to improve local living conditions, this small project provokes critical thinking regarding the new wave of rural development. Through an intimate collaboration among scholars, designers, makers, and villagers, nearby manufacturing workshops are given a chance to become reunited, and villagers enjoy unprecedented work opportunities. Both will help push the village toward hope.

Lukou Grameen Village Bank front view

Signage in front of building

Interior

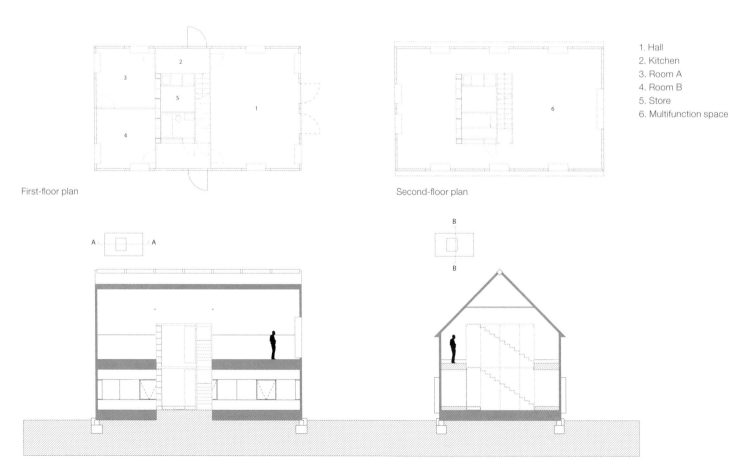

First-floor plan

Second-floor plan

1. Hall
2. Kitchen
3. Room A
4. Room B
5. Store
6. Multifunction space

Section A-A

Section B-B

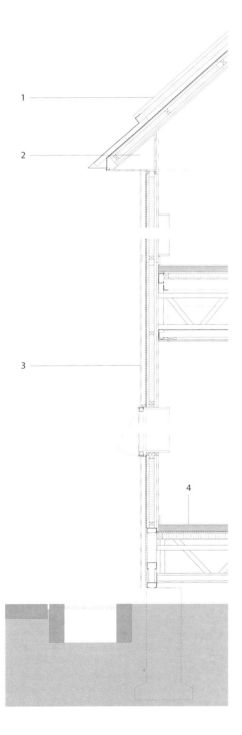

Local villagers during the construction

Detail

1. Roof construction:
Roof sandwich panel, 1820x1820 mm
joint panel framed with 40x40 mm timber
and covered with 9 mm plywood on
double face, 9 mm gypsum panel with
white painting

2. Ventilation eaves

3. Wall construction:
12 mm fiber cement board, 80 mm
ventilation gap, 1820x550 mm joint
panel framed with 40x40 mm timber and
covered with 3 mm polyester board on
double face, 9 mm gypsum panel with
white painting

4. Floor construction:
PVC floor, 100 mm lightweight precast
concrete panels, 1820x1820 mm joint
panel framed with 40x40 mm timber and
covered with 9 mm plywood on double
face, lightweight steel-truss structure

COMMUNITY PARTICIPATION: LOCAL WORKERS

Foundation and structure

Gao Niankuan
Lukou, Xinyi, Jiangsu

Huang Dianxi
Lukou, Xinyi, Jiangsu

Ji Shuyan
Lukou, Xinyi, Jiangsu

Su Xiaoying
Lukou, Xinyi, Jiangsu

Xu Junrong
Lukou, Xinyi, Jiangsu

Yin Yongkun
Lukou, Xinyi, Jiangsu

Yin Yongle
Lukou, Xinyi, Jiangsu

Metal processing

Yang Chuangwei
Yancheng, Jiangsu

Yin Yongchao
Lukou, Xinyi, Jiangsu

Shi Rongbing
Lukou, Xinyi, Jiangsu

Zhang Rong'e
Lukou, Xinyi, Jiangsu

Zhou Chun
Lukou, Xinyi, Jiangsu

Shi Rongjun
Lukou, Xinyi, Jiangsu

Funiture making · Utility works · Paintings

Shi Yang
Lukou, Xinyi, Jiangsu

Shi Ya
Lukou, Xinyi, Jiangsu

Liang Hao
Beigou, Xinyi, Jiangsu

Zhang Menghua
Beigou, Xinyi, Jiangsu

Peng Fei
Wangwo, Xinyi, Jiangsu

Chen Zongxia
Lukou, Xinyi, Jiangsu

Xu Hairong
Lukou, Xinyi, Jiangsu

Pavement

Gong Zhiwei
Lukou, Xinyi, Jiangsu

Han Yunxia
Lukou, Xinyi, Jiangsu

Huang Diancui
Lukou, Xinyi, Jiangsu

Lu Baodian
Lukou, Xinyi, Jiangsu

Lu Baoju
Lukou, Xinyi, Jiangsu

Wang Jiufu
Lukou, Xinyi, Jiangsu

Yin Changming
Lukou, Xinyi, Jiangsu

EFFICIENCY: CONSTRUCTION MANAGEMENT

6 November 2014

14 November 2014

15 November 2014

Foundation preparation

Steel structure arriving

Wood structure arriving

Funiture making

16 November 2014

17 November 2014

19 November 2014

Ground beam set up

Structure erection

Wall-panels assembly

Pipeline pre-buried

Roof-truss erection

20 November 2014

25 November 2014

27 November 2014

Beam-raising ceremony

Cold-bridge prevention

Roofing-panels assemby

Roofing-tile installation

Waterproof-layer installation

30 November 2014

9 December 2014

11 December 2014

Fiber cement boards installation

Pavement

Façade painting

Logo installation

CHAIMIDUO FARM RESTAURANT AND BAZAAR

Zhao Yang | Zhaoyang Architects

Location: Dali, Yunnan, China
Architect: Zhaoyang Architects
Design team: Yang Zhao, Peigen Shang
Restaurant interior designer: Xu Cai
Area: 647 square meters (site); 631 square meters (building)
Design period: May–September 2015
Construction period: June 2015–March 2016
Photography: Pengfei Wang

Site plan

The property was originally the site of an abandoned office facility located at the center of Dali Old Town, which included a traditional Bai-style timber structure, a bungalow constructed from brick and concrete, and a 200-square-meter courtyard. The property has been rented by a local lifestyle brand, Chaimiduo, and renovated for use as a farm restaurant, a farming supermarket, a gallery for handicrafts, and a space for the weekly Chaimiduo Bazaar.

The main idea of the renovation was to redefine the courtyard's four different sides with ad-hoc strategies. A second floor was added to the bungalow on the north side of the courtyard and topped with a traditional Bai-style tiled roof (in accordance with the design code of Dali Old Town). A steel pavilion in the shape of an irregular quadrilateral extrudes into the courtyard and connects the restaurant interior with the courtyard space. The pavilion was enveloped with bamboo to emphasize its

volume and to filter sunlight entering its interior. The bamboo façade is openable on the side facing the courtyard, allowing increased interaction during bazaar hours. The façade also extends upward, forming the banister for the terrace. The profile of the banister is tilted, directing the spatial orientation towards the preserved upper-floor façade and tiled roof of the neighboring timber structure.

The timber structure was constructed using traditional methods. We demolished the partition wall on the ground floor and the timber doors with wood lattices. Thus, the ground-floor space opens to the outside. We also added a system of bamboo sliding doors to the façade so that the openness can be adjusted. This bamboo system hides the original timber columns, introducing a new appearance that responds to the newly transformed open space. While completely canceling out the traditional image on the ground floor, this new façade also

highlights the more refined details on the preserved façade of the upper floor and tiled roof.

The southern side of the courtyard is the property's main entrance. We added a wedge-shaped pavilion to redefine this entrance space, providing shelter and transforming the spatial sequence. Bamboo is used as the ceiling in this section, producing a visual relationship with other bamboo façades and creating a more unified impression.

The west side of the courtyard has an iron fence adorned with lush local ivy, providing the property with soft, semitransparent protection. We simply added a wide timber platform that covers the flowerbed and can be used as a long bench or as a place for children to play during bazaar hours.

Chaimiduo Farm Restaurant and Bazaar interior views

Chaimiduo Farm Restaurant and Bazaar courtyard

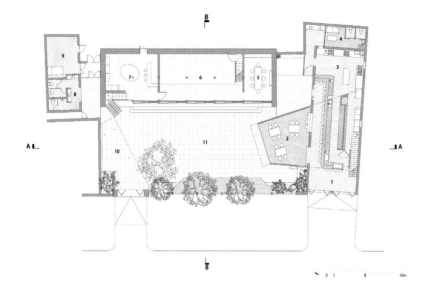

First-floor plan

1. Main entrance
2. Restaurant
3. Kitchen
4. Logistics rest
5. Teahouse
6. Gallery
7. Store
8. Restroom
9. Warehouse
10. Canopy and secondary entrance
11. Courtyard

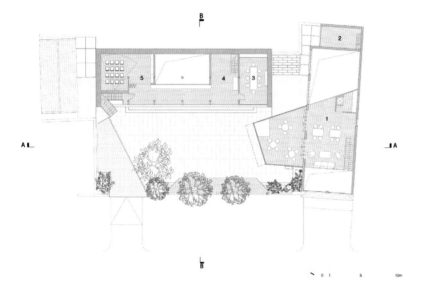

Second-floor plan

1. Restaurant
2. Logistics rest
3. Teahouse
4. Gallery
5. Projection room

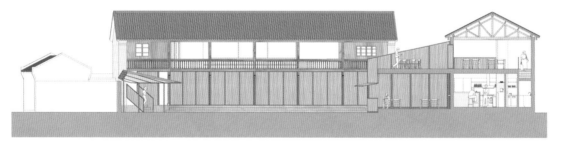

Section A-A

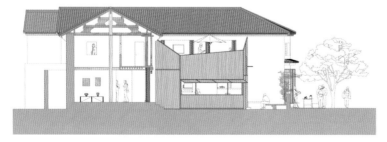

Section B-B

Interior of the timber-building gallery

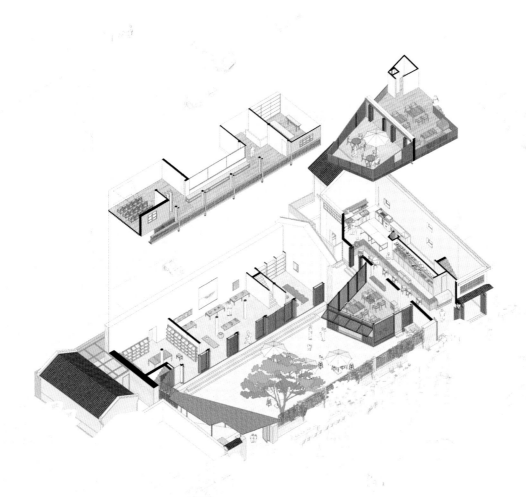

Axonometric drawing with program arrangement

SHIMEN BRIDGE

Xu Tiantian | DnA Architects

Location: Shimen Village, Songyang, Lishui, Zhejiang Province
Principal architect: Xu Tiantian
Design team: Xu Tiantian, Zhang Longxiao, Zhou Yang
Design period: October 2016
Construction period: September–December 2017

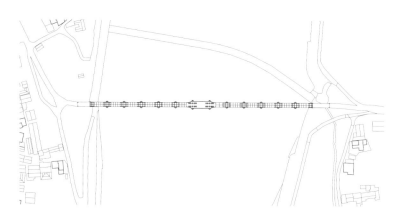

Site plan

Shimen Bridge acts as a landmark for villagers and connects the two villages located on the banks of Songyi River. While spatially it responds to Wang Jing Memorial Hall in Wang Village, the contrast between the natural landscape around the bridge and the sacred space of the Memorial Hall provokes reflections on such relationships between natural and culture. The bridge and the pavilion provide a space for villagers where they can feel the river. The form of the bridge was inspired by the traditional covered bridge in China. Based on the stone structure, we reduced the sense of closure by creating openings toward the river. The platform in the center of the bridge is also an ideal gathering space for villagers.

Shimen Bridge above Songyi River

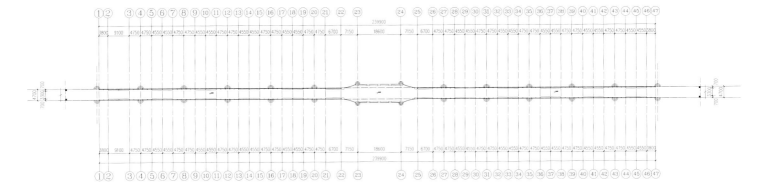

Plan

North elevation

Section

Bridge entrance

ZHONGGUAN VILLAGE TONGZI PEDESTRIAN BRIDGE

Fu Yingbin | China New Rural Planning and Design

Location: Zhongguan Village, Tongzi Province, Guizhou, China
Principal architect: Fu Yingbin, China New Rural Planning and Design
Design team: Haoran Zhang, Lu Yan, Yang Liu, Daoxing Zhou
Design period: March 2016
Construction period: August 2016

Site plan

Zhongguan Village, located in the remote mountains of Guizhou, China, suffers from limited transportation and a declining economy. Flue-cured tobacco planting is the village's core industry. The village is currently facing serious decline. With the support of China's poverty alleviation policies, the designer transformed and renewed many public facilities in the village in the role of collaborator. This was an attempt to realize a comprehensive embrace of life and culture and explore a new avenue for rural rejuvenation with acupuncture-style micro interventions.

The village is divided in two by a river. In rainy season, the rising river would flood the old single-board wooden bridge spanning the river and cut off access. Building a bridge was significant not only to restoring traffic, but also to rebuilding mankind's relationship with villages and nature. Since villagers were only pro-

ficient in very basic construction techniques and time was of the essence, it was thus necessary to develop a stable and simple method of achieving the goals. We chose to form solid and flexible piers by stacking gabions, a mature material. In this way, villagers were able to conduct rapid construction themselves. In addition, over time, plants will grow through the stone cages and deposit sand in the cracks. Welding is a common, mature construction technique. We purchased finished steel directly to complete the bridge structure and did the welding work on-site. Finished metal scaffolding partitions were used for the bridge floor. These are not only strong and corrosion-resistant, but also allow travelers to see the river flowing beneath through the steel mesh. Unlike in conventional industrial metal bridges, bamboo was used for the handrails and lampposts. Entire bamboo stems were installed on the bridge at random intervals in a natural, visual language. The

towering bamboo lampposts visually echo the reeds in the river, romantic and poetic, like a row of candles in the valley.

The construction process was a collaboration between the designer and the villagers. The designer humbly adjusted the plan according to the constantly evolving situation. Thus, the end of the design process corresponded with the end of the construction process. Since ancient times, villagers have believed that the construction of roads and bridges is a great event that will benefit posterity. Village elders chose the installation time and held a ceremony, then the villagers raised and installed the steel beams together. This bridge, built by the villagers themselves, brought them together.

Overall view

Children playing on the bridge

Elevation

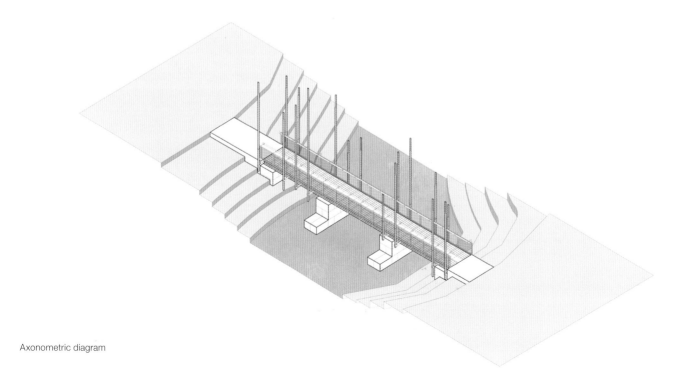

Axonometric diagram

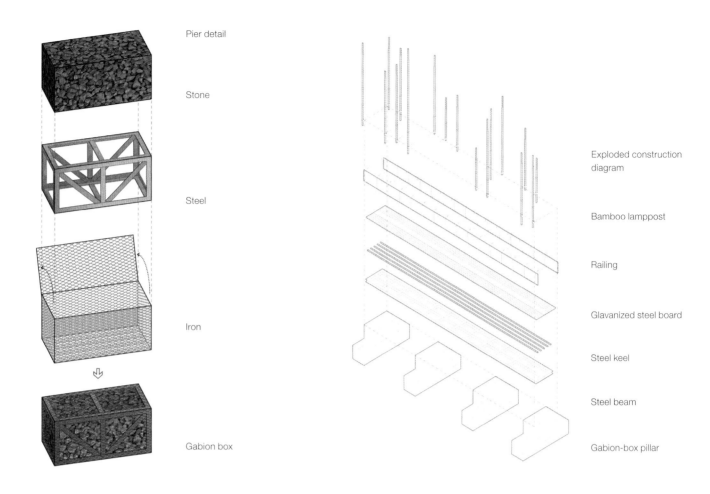

Pier detail

Stone

Steel

Iron

Gabion box

Exploded construction diagram

Bamboo lamppost

Railing

Glavanized steel board

Steel keel

Steel beam

Gabion-box pillar

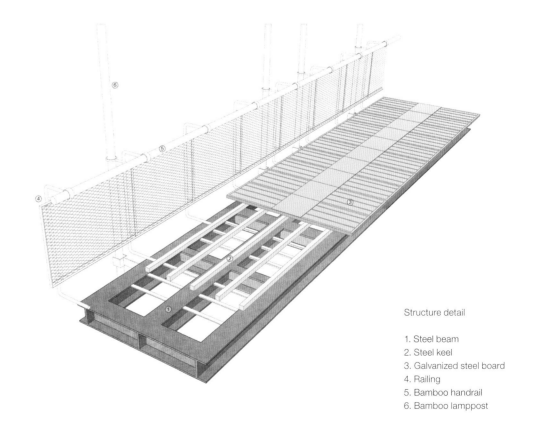

Structure detail

1. Steel beam
2. Steel keel
3. Galvanized steel board
4. Railing
5. Bamboo handrail
6. Bamboo lamppost

FUTUR

拓

Turning from the world factory to the world market, China's countryside is becoming the frontier of global economics participators and even innovators. Thanks to globalized mobility, internet, and technology, the grand future of China's countryside can be envisioned: more intensive urban/rural collaboration, growing hybrid industry, and multiple business patterns. What China's countryside has already accomplished is no less than what the city has achieved, if not surpassing it. When it comes to making vital industry chains of e-commerce, logistics and distribution, online finance, community services, and so on, the countryside has become the incubated land with its labor and regional advantages.

Being a rural community center, Philip F. Yuan's **In Bamboo** is simultaneously futuristic and traditional. With computational design methods and digital prefabrication technology, the project has reached an efficiency and complexity as well as a balance between local craft and cutting-edge technologies. Yuan also designed **Cloud Village** in the garden outside the Pavilion of China. Robotically 3D printed with modified plastic material, Cloud Village represents a reflection of the contemporary environment crisis in China's coun-tryside as well as proposing a new thinking on building materials and sustainability. While Cunkou, the public space located at the entrance of a village, is a typological reference for the project, at Venice, Cloud Village will act as a public space for visitors with its cubic volumes and the geometrical configuration of the roof. The name "cloud" refers both to its free-form roof and the

cloud technology of the internet, which also breeds new architectural types and development models of the countryside in China. Inside the pavilion, Li Zhenyu's photography series **Village Air Reading** is exhibited. Zhang Lei's **Shitang Internet Conference Center** is inspired by historic types, such as the commune auditorium and the vegetable greenhouse, and attempts to reconstruct their spatiality for an internet conference center. Drawing Architecture Studio depicts the phenomenon of **Taobao Village** in China. Taobao Village, which is a term put forward by AliResearch in 2009, is a village where the number of households that are engaged in e-commerce has reached a substantial amount. As internet and logistic services have greatly compressed and flattened geographical distance, Taobao Village proposes an opportunity for the future of the countryside.

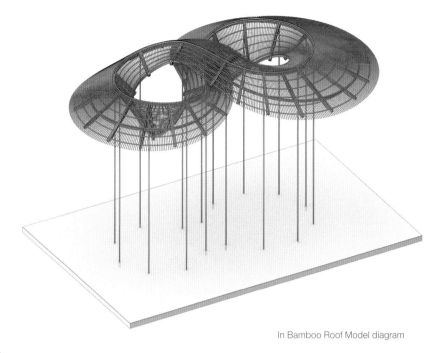

In Bamboo Roof Model diagram

IN BAMBOO ROOF MODEL

Architect: Philip F. Yuan
Fabricator: Shanghai Wen Zhu Model Design Co., Ltd.
Area: 6 square meters (3x2x2 meters)
Materials: Wood and steel plates

In Bamboo is a rural construction project designed and fabricated by Philip F. Yuan and his team at the beginning of 2017. The project is a multifunctional rural community cultural center with provisions for exhibitions, hosting conferences, community gathering, as well as dining and recreation. It integrates the site with the surrounding villages, traditional construction techniques with prefabricated industrialization, which is typified in its roof design and fabrication.

The gestural interweaving roof is a construction of many prefabricated parts delivered to the site ready for quick assembly. The Möbius-shaped roof is supported by a 70 percent, light prefabricated steel frame and finished with traditional ceramic tiles. The architecture, landscaping, and interior were completed in 52 days. Using digitally pre-fabricated structural wood construction we were able to reduce waste while increasing the speed of installation.

The relationships of inside and outside, bamboo and tile, and new and old are able to be experienced in the infinite shape (∞) of the roof. The new definition offered for traditional paradigms and the rethinking of rural and urban issues provide a lens for thinking about the meaning of architecture in the present time.

The site is located on two adjacent, mismatched land parcels. In each of these parcels we drew one large circle; these two circles came together determining the large contour for our building while still preserving the surrounding bamboo forest and trees. Within this new boundary we sought to maximize the continuity, horizontality, and ductility of the space. The floating roof provides the widest possible view of the pristine natural vista outside. At its best, the visitor is left with a sense of merging with nature itself.

The dwellings nearby have much to say about the character of this location; they speak the language of local material and enduring climate responses. The double curved geometry of our roof design is difficult to achieve using a continuous material. A way forward was found using gray roof tiles discovered in the local architecture of Daoming. On the roof of our building the tile is like a pixel, computed to describe the subtle geometric complexity of this continuous roof. In this way the tiles became the intermediary linking vernacular building language with abstract geometry.

Robotic fabrication of roof structure

IN BAMBOO

Philip F. Yuan | Archi-Union Architects Co., Ltd.

Location: Daoming Town, Chongzhou, Sichuan Province, China
Architect: Shanghai Archi-Union Architecture Design Co., Ltd.
Digital fabricator: Shanghai Fab-Union Architectural Technology and Digital Fabrication Co., Ltd,
Principal architect: Philip F. Yuan
Design team: Alex Han, Kong Xiangping, Yang Bing, Zhu Tianrui
Interior designers: Wen Qinhao, Chen Xiaoming, Tang Jingyan
Structural designers: Wang Jing, Li Lei, Liang Chen, Zhou Qiang
Electromechanical engineering consultants: Liu Yong, Yu Ying, Zhou Qiang
Timber structural construction: Suzhou Crownhomes Co., Ltd.
Digital fabrication: Zhang Wen, Zhang Liming, He Sizhong
Area: 1800 square meters
Design period: August 2016–April 2017
Construction period: December 2016–April 2017
Photography: Lin Bian

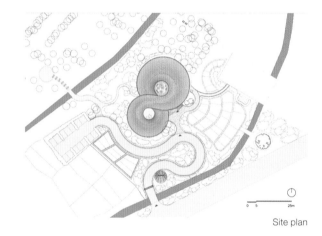

Site plan

Archi-Union Architects from China have created a rural community center in Daoming Town supported by a 70 percent prefabricated timber-frame structure. The center is a configuration of two patios covered by a Möbius roof finished with traditional ceramic tiles. The project is simultaneously futuristic and traditional in its approach.

The center is in a suburb of Daoming Town, Chongzhou County, well known for its extensive bamboo-weaving tradition. As the first demonstration project in this rural area, the center is designed for the purposes of hosting bamboo-weaving craft events, providing a hub for cultural sharing, and for accommodating other multifunction activities.

Archi-Union Architects began this project with the intention of extending traditional crafts and inspiration stemming from an ancient Chinese poem. The work attempts to integrate new life generated by the activities at the center with the original site, the surrounding villages, and natural ecological resources.

"Building can only try to start a dialogue with earth, while plants belong to the earth. We were trying our best to maintain everything, and keep the most stay still," said Principal Architect Philip F. Yuan.

People will experience a strong feeling of Chinese poetic beauty when entering the building. It shapes space in the manner of a Chinese garden. Layers and transparency create an interaction between people and light.

Traditional materials are used in an intelligent manner throughout the project. Since traditional bamboo weaving was not appropriate for the architectural structure, it instead appears as a façade-texture wrapping the exterior of the building. Similarly, clay, ceramic, timber, and tile have all been applied with sensitivity where found suitable.

This community center is also an avant garde exploration of how to integrate new construction technology with local crafts in the era of digital humanities. The project integrates parametric design, traditional construction techniques, and contemporary prefabrication industrialization. The high efficiency afforded by prefabrication made the 52-day construction period possible. In that time, all of the main building construction, interior, and landscape site work was completed.

In Bamboo night view

"We actually need to bring something urban and futuristic to our countries, instead of simply imitating. If our future countries' industrialized factories can be equipped with advanced industrialization approaches and instruments, like robotic construction and digital industry, it would certainly rouse a significant industrial upgrading. We can already foresee it in this project," concluded Philip F. Yuan.

Aerial view of In Bamboo

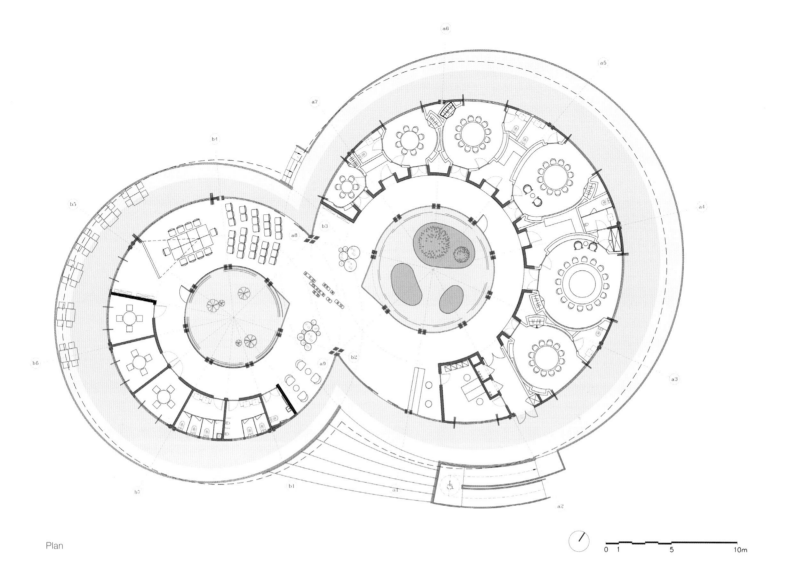

Plan

0 1   5   10m

Roof construction process

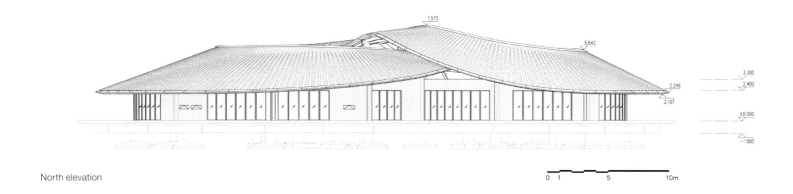

North elevation

0 1   5   10m

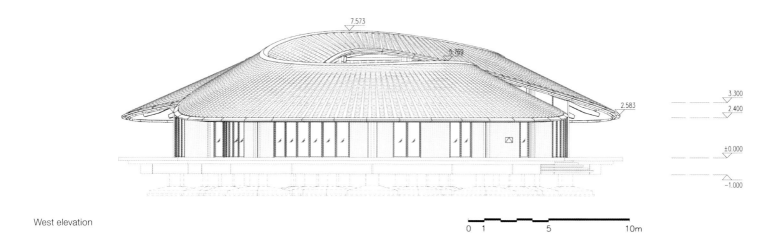

West elevation

0 1   5   10m

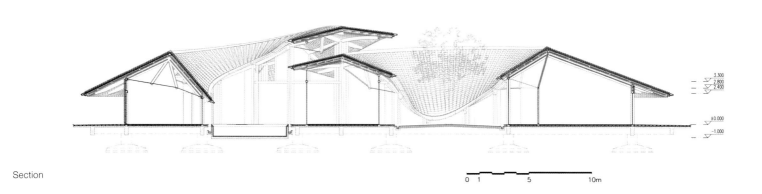

Section

0 1   5   10m

In Bamboo at dusk

Locals weaving bamboo under the shaded space

Roof structure detail

View of restaurant

Inner courtyard

CLOUD VILLAGE

Philip F. Yuan | Archi-Union Architects Co., Ltd.

Location: Daoming Town, Chongzhou, Sichuan Province, China
Architect: Shanghai Archi-Union Architecture Design Co., Ltd.
Digital fabricator: Shanghai Fab-Union Architectural Technology and Digital Fabrication Co., Ltd.
Principal architect: Philip F. Yuan
Design team: Alex Han, Kong Xiangping, Yang Bing, Zhu Tianrui
Interior designers: Wen Qinhao, Chen Xiaoming, Tang Jingyan
Structural designers: Wang Jing, Li Lei, Liang Chen, Zhou Qiang
Electromechanical engineering consultants: Liu Yong, Yu Ying, Zhou Qiang
Timber structural construction: Suzhou Crownhomes Co., Ltd.
Digital fabrication: Zhang Wen, Zhang Liming, He Sizhong
Area: 1800 square meters
Design period: August 2016–April 2017
Construction period: December 2016–April 2017
Photography: Lin Bian

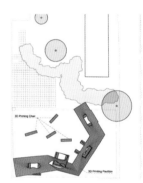

Site plan

Cloud Village outside Pavilion of China at the 16th International Architecture Exhibition of La Biennale di Venezia will be built with modified plastic by the robotic printing technology developed by Philip F. Yuan and his team.

Cloud Village reflects the contemporary reality of Chinese countryside through its semiotic performance of materiality. The recycled plastic material of the pavilion indicates the environmental crisis of the Chinese countryside, and establishes a critical rethinking of sustainable spatial production for the future.

The spatial distribution of Cloud Village is an abstract representation of rural everday life. It seeks the possibility of establishing a new relation between the individual and the collective under the circumstance of globalization, to establish a new identity for the dwellers.

The pavilion contains four semi-enclosed cubic objects that are organized together by a shared linear roof. The cubic objects are standing on the ground and oriented towards slightly different directions. Meanwhile, each of the objects is merged with the linear roof in a unique way to produce a special condition of roof covering. Standing in those cubic spaces, the occupant could experience highly diversified dialogues to the surrounding view, to the sky, to the earth, and to each other eventually.

The distribution of the cubic objects, together with the geometrical configuration of the roof, creates a free space embracing the building entrance, and turning the whole pavilion into a community. As all the private spaces completely open to this central public space, the boundary between them is only defined by the roof. Consequently, there are no clear

distinctions between private and public as well as individual and collective. In the end, this kind of spatial uncertainty produces a latent atmosphere for the site to destabilize the identity of each occupant.

The fabrication of Cloud Village adopts a new model of production based on an integrated robotic factory. The new production system offers the possibility for the architect to combine various tools into an operation network, and to establish a new authority of design, which is not referring to the final product, but based on the intelligence embedded in the production process.

Cloud Village

The pavilion aims to combine structural performance-based design methodology with robotic fabrication technology in a highly integrated process. The form of the pavilion is optimized by adopting a series of topological algorithm to enhance the overall structure performance. By turning the flat roof into the waved geometry, the structural stiffness of the cantilever roofs is highly increased.

The robotic -fabrication logic has been incorporated into the formation process. Then the continuous geometry of the pavilion is pixelated into a series of discrete components, each of which contains a unique crystalized printing toolpath. As the stress on the overall form would be distributed into the pixels of the grid system, the entire network has to be modified into five types of different densities according to different structural performance

along the surface. The denser zones are used for bearing the load of the structure while the zones of less density provide longer spans used for covering a greater area. In the end, based on the support of digital design and robotic construction technology, Cloud Village demonstrates the full integration of structural performance analysis technology with the designed form, and establishes a new model of production in building industry.

Under the cloud

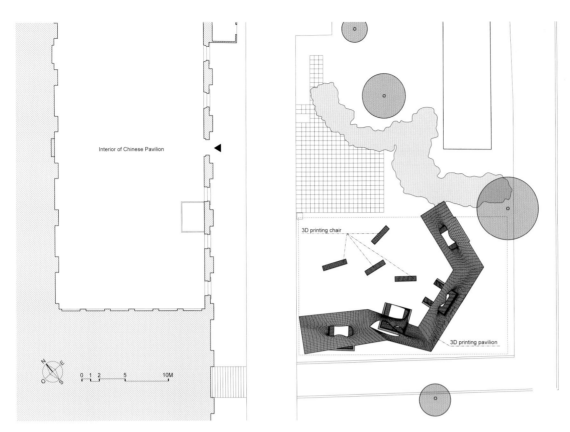

Plan

Cloud Village

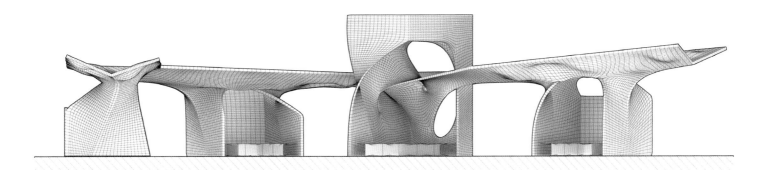

Elevation

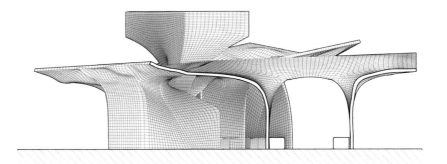

Section

Robotic 3D printing with modified plastic

TAOBAO VILLAGE, SMALLACRE CITY

Li Han + Hu Yan | Drawing Architecture Studio

Project team: Li Han, Hu Yan, Zhang Xintong, Ji Jiawei, Liu Liyuan, Yuan Ruizhe, Ye Zichen
Medium: Digital drawing
Project completion: 2018

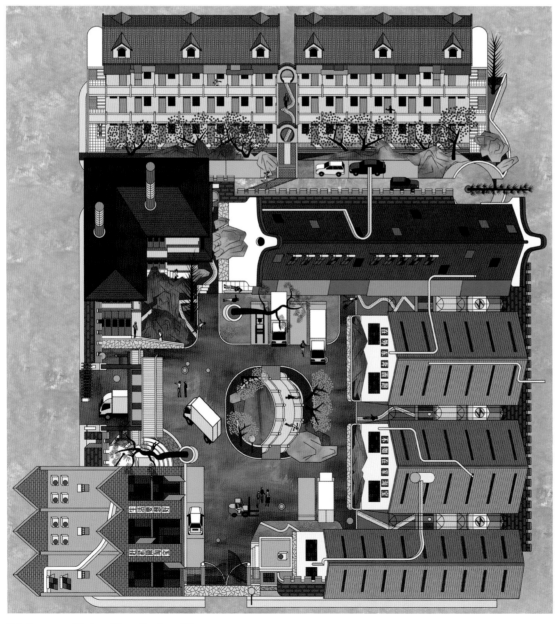

Exterior scene of Taobao Village, Smallacre City

With the rapid development of the internet and logistics, Chinese countryside is now tied into urban development. The transformation in the relationship between the city and the countryside is manifested in Taobao Village, a term put forward by AliResearch.[1] Taobao Village functions as both a return to the countryside and a step out of the countryside. As a canonical agrarian utopia in the U.S., Frank Lloyd Wright's Broadacre City relates to the Chinese Taobao Village in various aspects despite their fundamental differences. "In the future, the city will disappear," such was Wright's prophecy. Yet, the city and the countryside still exist as two poles of human settlements. However, in contemporary China, the city and the countryside are more than ever connected thanks to the internet. From this perspective, Taobao Village, Smallacre City is a realist critique and Chinese interpretation of Broadacre City.

Based on visual materials collected from Taobao Villages, the project presents a figurative Taobao Village and its related facilities based on Wright's master plan, thus producing a clear connection to Broadacre City. The road structure and infrastructure layout from Broadacre City are kept the same and programs from Taobao Villages are added. The panorama is composed of two mirrored squares whose program and circulation are identical. The square on the right depicts an exterior scene. One depicts the exterior scene of Taobao Village and the other depicts the interiors through different representational techniques.

While the gigantic Broadacre City is measured with the acre, the panorama is planned according to the mu, a unit of land area used in China. The basic planning unit in Taobao Village, Smallacre City is a half mu (about 300 square meters). As such, this is also where its name Half Mu City originates.[2]

1. According to AliResearch, Alibaba Group's research arm, a Taobao Village is a cluster of rural e-tailers within an administrative village that meets the following criteria: 1) Residents started in e-commerce spontaneously primarily with the use of Taobao Marketplace; 2) Total annual e-commerce transaction volume is at least RMB10 million (USD$1.6 million); 3) At least 10 percent of village households actively engage in e-commerce or at least 100 active online shops have been opened by villagers.

2. Smallacre City in Chinese is referenced to as 半亩城 (Half Mu City), which is more directly connected to its planning unit.

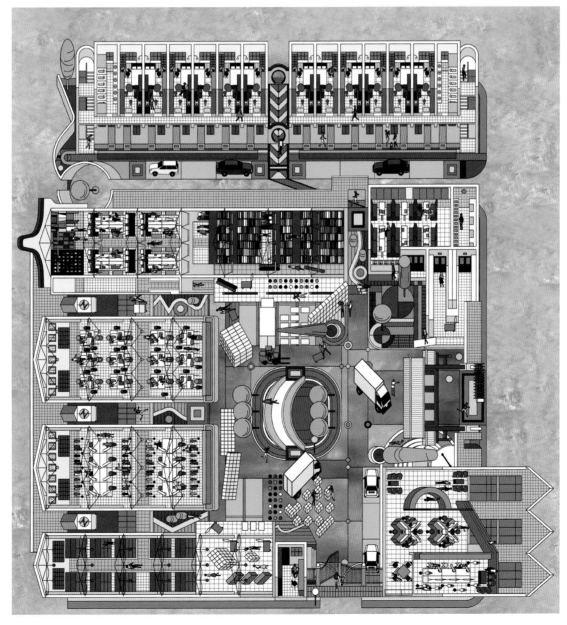

Inerior scene of Taobao Village, Smallacre City

SHITANG INTERNET CONFERENCE CENTER

Zhang Lei | AZL Architects

Location: Nanjing, Jiangsu Province
Architects: Zhong Huaying, Zhang Lei, AZL Architects
Design team: Zhong Huaying, Zhang Lei, Xi Hong
Cooperative organization: Institute of Architecture Design and Planning Co., Ltd. of Nanjing University, Shanghai Tongji Steel Structure Technology, Ltd.
Area: 3000 square meters
Project completion: October 2016
Photography: Yao Li, Hou Bowen

Site plan

The trend of modernization and urbanization in rural development inevitably requires the introduction of new types of multi-functional buildings, such as Shitang Internet Conference Center. Taking the commune auditorium and the vegetable greenhouse as the original form, Shitang Village Project in Jiangning tries to reconstruct public buildings in a rural context. Efforts have been made to rapidly build a system through industrialization, utilizing a prefabricated super-slender column structure, selectively applying technology to eliminate weakened and materialized buildings, restoring the primitive feeling of rural villages, and rejuvenating construction practice in an extremely short time period in rural villages.

Historic architecture types in rural China: commune auditorium and greenhouse.

East colonnade

Entrance and façade

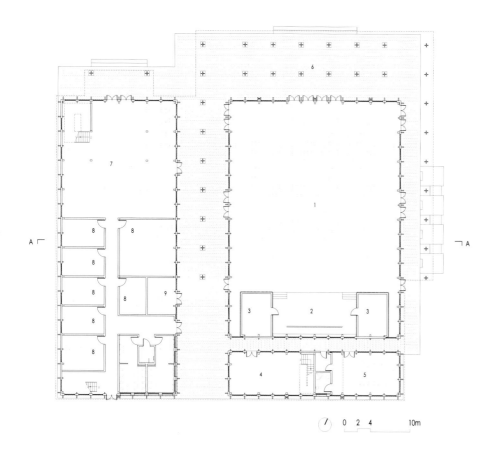

First-floor plan

1. Multifunctional hall
2. Stage
3. Equipment room
4. Storage
5. VIP lounge
6. Colonnade
7. Exhibition hall
8. Office
9. Fire control room
10. Activity room

0 2 4   10m

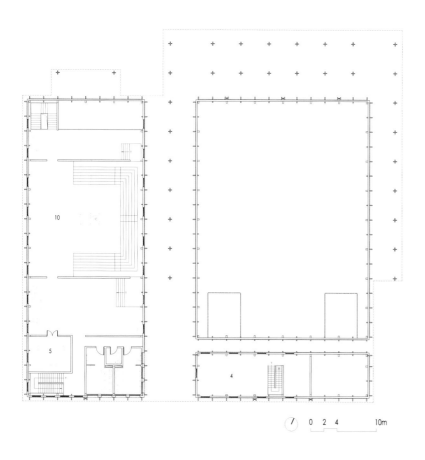

Second-floor plan

1. Multifunction hall
2. Stage
3. Equipment room
4. Storeroom
5. VIP lounge
6. Colonnade
7. Exhibition hall
8. Office
9. Fire control room
10. Activity room

0 2 4   10m

North elevation

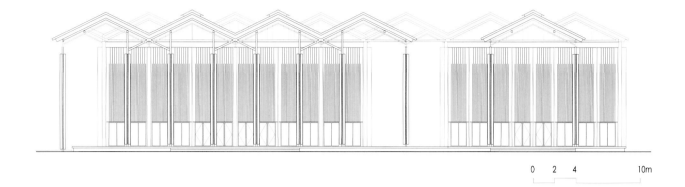

0 2 4   10m

East elevation

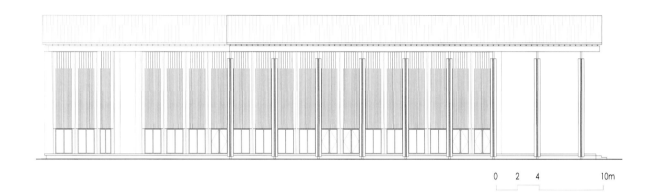

0 2 4   10m

Section A-A

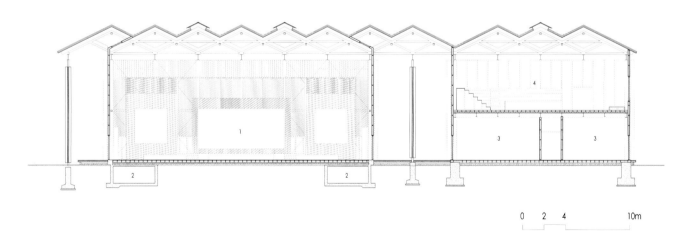

0 2 4   10m

1. Multifunction hall
2. Equipment room
3. Office
4. Activity room

East elevation in the morning

Conference room

Roof detail:

1. Wave tile:
4 mm SBS self-adhesive modified asphalt waterproof membrane
11.9 mm OSB board
12 mm calcium silicate board
120×50×20 mm galvanized C-shape steel at 600 mm spacing
120 mm level A non-combustible rock-wool insulation board
2 mm gray aluminum board
50×300 mm grating
150×150 mm steel tube
2. 150×150 mm steel tube
3. 140×140 mm prestressed thin column
4. 50×200 mm carbonized wood

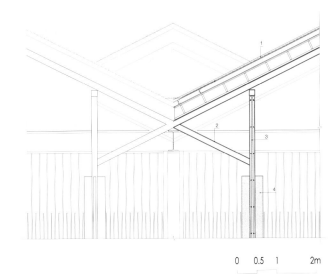

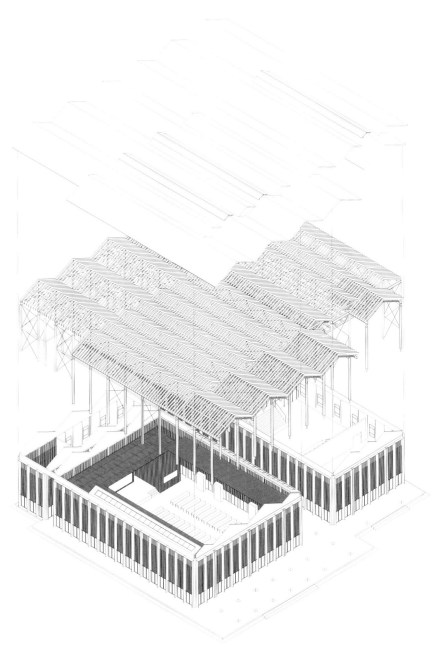

Exploded axonometric drawing

To share Chinese architects and architecture with the world

by deepening an appreciation of
Chinese architectural traditions and trends.

Something you shall know about CAUP

The College of Architecture and Urban Planning of Tongji University:

Located in Shanghai, China
Founded in 1952

2018 QS World University Ranking by Subject
– Architecture / Built Environment: **18**

3 Departments: Architecture, Urban Planning, Landscape Architecture

1 Center: Built Environment Technology Center

4 Undergraduate programs: Architecture, Urban and Rural Planning, Landscape Architecture, Historic Building Protection Engineering

3 Master and doctoral programs: Architecture, Urban and Rural Planning, Landscape Architecture

18 International dual degree programs: 1 undergraduate programs, 17 graduate programs

69 Courses taught in English

237 Full-time faculty members and researchers
61 Full-time staff, including:
88 Full professors and research fellows
91 Associate professors, associate research fellows, and senior engineers
11 Research specialists from the Institute for Advanced Study
14 Postdoctoral researchers
219 Adjunct faculty members and researchers, including:
115 International professors

5 Academic journals, including:
3 In Chinese: *Urban Planning Forum*, *Time+Architecture*, *Heritage Architecture*
2 In English: *Built Heritage*, *Landscape and Urban Planning*

Into the new century, CAUP begun to place emphasis on four academic directions, Eco-city, Green Architecture, Heritage Preservation, and Digital Design, to form new strong disciplines based on the existing development, and to evolve new branches of advanced disciplines by constructing cross-disciplinary platforms.

As a college with academic responsibilities, CAUP will join hands with students to explore new knowledge and to actively embrace the unknown new era.

For this purpose, CAUP would like to build a P-to-P platform for students, which is very precious for the young who are already accustomed to the internet. The platform includes but is not limited to:

People to People
Student to student, student to teacher, and teacher to teacher
People to Paper
Papers, books, experiments, topics, plus more.
People to Project
Exhibitions, performances, lectures, installations, plus more.
People to Practice
Conditions for real-world design practices
Peoples to Peoples
Global collaborations, professional networks, and interdisciplinary channels

WELCOME TO EACH ONE OF YOU WHO IS YOUNG, AND WHO WILL STAY YOUNG FOREVER!
WELCOME TO SHANGHAI, WELCOME TO CAUP OF TONGJI UNIVERSITY!

TONGJI UNIVERSITY
CAUP

TJAD

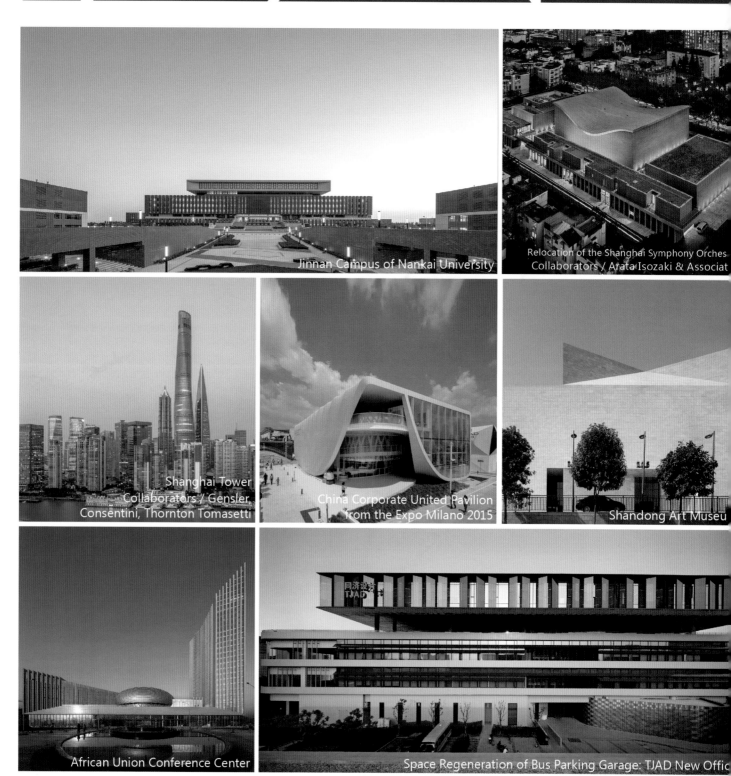

Jinnan Campus of Nankai University

Relocation of the Shanghai Symphony Orches
Collaborators / Arata Isozaki & Associat

Shanghai Tower
Collaborators / Gensler
Consentini, Thornton Tomasetti

China Corporate United Pavilion
from the Expo Milano 2015

Shandong Art Museu

African Union Conference Center

Space Regeneration of Bus Parking Garage: TJAD New Offic

Tongji Architectural Design (Group) Co., Ltd.

同济 设计 TJAD

🌐 www.tjad.cn
✆ 8621-65987788
🖷 8621-65985121
📍 No.1230 Siping Road, Shanghai
✉ mh@tjad.cn

Tongji Architectural Design (Group) Co., Ltd.(TJAD) was founded
1958 and has now developed into a well-known large-scale desig
consulting group with more than 4000 employees. It is one of the lead
ing design institutes in China with the most comprehensive range
disciplines available in the country, allowing it to develop many types
design projects. Based on the 2017 annual revenue, TJAD ranked top
for the civil architectural design enterprise and number 10 on the list
Top 60 Engineering Design Enterprises of China 2017 by Constructi
Times and ENR jointly.

上海同济城市规划设计研究院
SHANGHAI TONGJI URBAN PLANNING & DESIGN INSTITUTE

Shanghai Tongji Urban Planning and Design Institute was established in 1994, formerly Urban Planning & Architecture Studio in 1982. **TJUPDI** is a collaboration of industry, academics, and research, linking state needs and incubating academic company. **TJUPDI** is insisting in sustainable service providing suitable innovation and cultural diversity.

UNESCO Honourable Mention Asia-Pacific Awards for Cultural Heritage Conservation, 2016: The World Bank Loan Project-Liu Ancestral Hall Preservation and Renovation of San Mentang Village, Tianzhu County (September 2013–August 2014)

2. Liu Ancestral Hall after the renovation

Guizhou Province

Project Location

Southeast of Guizhou Province

Fig. 1. Project location

Fig. 3. Bird's-eye view of San Mentang Village

UNESCO
Asia-Pacific Awards for
Cultural Heritage
Conservation
— 2016 —

The preservation of Liu Ancestral Hall is notable for the application of a rigorous scientific approach. Dating to the Qing Dynasty with further embellishment during the time of the Republic of China, the hall had declined into poor structural condition with damage to its surfaces, including its renowned decorative stucco façade. The project's proponents successfully carried out non-intrusive investigation of the building fabric, systematic testing of possible solutions and meticulous conservation interventions. In reviving a significant historic building for on-going use by Dong ethnic group villagers and to attract outside visitors, the project contributes to a larger initiative to protect and promote Guizhou's diverse cultural and natural heritage.

Honourable Mention

The World Bank Loan- Guizhou Cultural and Natural Heritage Protection and Development - Liu Ancestral Hall Preservation and Renovation Project of Sanmentang Village
Guizhou Province, China

Owner:
Liu's Family

Individuals Responsible for the Project:
Jian Zhou; Guangming Yan; Guang Li

Architect / Designer / Consultant:
Mr. Shibing Dai; Mr. Bin Shi; Mr. Yingchun Fu; Mr. Kunping Zhou; Ms. Huaiyun Kou; Mr.Chengbao Zhang; Ms. Lin Wang; Ms. Zhen Liu; Ms. Gesa Schwantes; Mr.Nongbing Gong; Mr. Chonghe Rao

General Contractor:
The Provincial Project Management Office of the World Bank Loan-Guizhou Cultural and Natural Heritage Protection and Development; Tongji University, Shanghai Tongji Urban Planning and Design Institute; Easen International Co.,Ltd.; Guizhou Baoli Chinese Traditional Building Construction Co., Ltd.

Fig. 4. Bird's-eye view of Liu Ancestral Hall

Floor area: 200m²   Roof: 240m²   Wall: 510m²   Project cost: USD$120,000

天华 Tianhua

20 YEARS FOR BETTER CITIES AND LIFESTYLE

Urban Planning | Architecture | Landscape | Interior

www.thape.com.cn